To Dad
Xmas 95.
Love You Lots.

xxx

THE GASTRODROME COOKBOOK

THE GASTRODROME COOKBOOK

Rory Ross

Introduction by Sir Terence Conran

•

Special Photography by Roger Stowell

PAVILION

For Isabella

First published in Great Britain in 1995 by
PAVILION BOOKS LIMITED
26 Upper Ground, London SE19PD
Text copyright © Rory Ross 1995
Introduction copyright © Sir Terence Conran 1995
Recipes copyright © Conran Restaurants 1995
Special photographs copyright © Roger Stowell 1995
For full picture acknowledgements see page 160

The moral right of the author has been asserted.
Designed by Bernard Higton

A CIP catalogue record for this book
is available from the British Library.

ISBN 1 85793 6949

Printed and bound in Italy by Graphicom

Recipes written and tested by Wendy Shuttleworth
from those supplied by Lucy Crabb (Blue Print Café),
David Burke (Le Pont de la Tour), Louis Loizia
(Cantina del Ponte) and Rod Eggleston (Butlers Wharf Chop-house).
Home economy and styling by Gillian McLaurin

This book may be ordered by post
direct from the publisher. Please contact
the Marketing Department.
But try your bookshop first.

Those recipes marked with ❤ are suitable for vegetarians.

CONTENTS

INTRODUCTION

I have always held the firm conviction that good design improves the quality of everyone's life. At Butlers Wharf, the site of the Gastrodrome in London, I have had the opportunity to put this belief to the test, perhaps more thoroughly than in any other project in which I have ever been involved.

Butlers Wharf is on the south bank of the River Thames and in the shadow of Tower Bridge. From the moment I saw the site in the late seventies, I believed the area was ripe for renewal and revival, that it could be a wonderfully cosmopolitan alternative to Covent Garden. As I found out more about the area and thought about submitting a planning proposal, the opportunity for a restaurant along the riverfront seemed too good to miss.

Initially, I had planned a single, major restaurant and café as part of the redevelopment. But as my involvement grew, so did my ambitions. The first restaurant to open was the Blue Print Café, above the Design Museum, and its success disproved City wisdom that no one would travel any distance 'just' to get good food. Since then, three more restaurants – Le Pont de la Tour, Cantina del Ponte and the Butlers Wharf Chop-house – have opened, along with a Food Store, Wine Merchant, Smoked Fish and Crustacea Shop, Chop-house Shop and Oils and Spice Shop; there is also a bakery supplying the restaurants and the Food Store. Hence the Gastrodrome – a centre of gastronomic excellence. The restaurants and shops, which are all, I hope, pretty good in their own right, work together to create something even greater than the sum of its parts: an eating experience unique in London. A chefs' school, which I hope will open towards the end of 1995, will add yet another element to the commitment to seriously good food.

The Gastrodrome is a good example, I think, of designing a better style of life; the scale of the venture, its ambience and design make Butlers Wharf, with its riverside views, a memorable and thoroughly enjoyable place to visit. There is not a single detail that has not come under the scrutiny of a designer, from the planning of the kitchen and the design of the interiors through the furniture, china, glass and staff uniforms to the way in which the food is presented and the graphics used on the menus, wine lists and even the style of the bills. Most importantly, all these elements have come together to create a better style of life for everyone who comes here to eat; and in doing that, the Gastrodrome has played an important – and profitable – role in the rejuvenation of a previously forgotten and derelict part of London.

This book captures the experience of visiting the Gastrodrome: a combination of delicious food, attentive and knowledgeable staff, thoughtful design and a spectacular location with glamorous views of the City and Tower Bridge. Additionally, the selection of mouthwatering recipes allows you to recreate something of the culinary excellence in your own kitchen.

Terence Conran

A GASTRONOMIC WONDERLAND

Gastrodrome?' The name was invented for a unique family of restaurants and food shops in Butlers Wharf, an eleven-acre rectangle of land tucked under the southeast rampart of Tower Bridge in London. Each of the restaurants that make up this group – Le Pont de la Tour Restaurant, Bar and Grill, the Butlers Wharf Chop-house, Cantina del Ponte and the Blue Print Café – is inspired by a different school or regional styles of cooking: French, British, Italian, Irish, Mediterranean and New World.

Culinary exotica are nothing new to Butlers Wharf. In a previous incarnation, the area was a teeming entrepôt where merchants and adventurers unloaded clippers packed with tea chests from India and China, barrels of wine from France, crates of cardamom pods from the East Indies and cocoa beans from Africa. The last remnants of Butlers Wharf's spice heritage disappeared only in 1994 when Butlers, Grinders & Operators moved out, but on hot days a pungent zephyr still circulates among the wharfs and warehouses.

The Gastrodrome is a foodie's heaven, offering the finest produce, including lobster and a range of olives.

The first floor terrace of the Blue Print Café enjoys spectacular views of the River Thames and Tower Bridge.

From the remains of one swashbuckling merchant empire has risen another, altogether different in its subtle, witty blending of food, design and art, but equally buccaneering in style. The Gastrodrome remains true to the pioneering spirit of that lost age. Where raw exotic foodstuffs were once brought eagerly ashore, the same ingredients are now exquisitely purveyed in humming restaurants: at Le Pont de la Tour, Crab and Saffron Tart; at the Blue Print Café, Hot Spiced Mussels with Coconut and Coriander; at Cantina del Ponte, Fig and Cinnamon Tart; and at the Butlers Wharf Chop-house, Steak, Kidney and Oyster Pudding.

The upholstered banquettes add a splash of colour to the design scheme of Cantina del Ponte.

Adding depth and width to the gastronomic coverage are five shops – the Food Store, the Chop-house Shop, the Wine Merchant, the Smoked Fish and Crustacea Shop, the Oils and Spices Shop – which sell everyday staples such as bread, eggs and milk, as well as speciality items: regional wines, the daily catch and almost every condiment under the sun. There is also a *Salon Privé* at Le Pont de la Tour for private parties.

This Xanadu of the tastebud puts food at centre-stage. Specifically its aim is to celebrate the choosing, buying, cooking, presentation and eating of food; to make it fun, accessible and enjoyable. According to the rubric, the Gastrodrome is aimed at 'bon viveurs; gastronomes; foodies; and down-to-earth greedy people, devoted to food and wine'.

The 100 or so recipes in this book are picked by the four chefs at the Gastrodrome, and range from the basics to more substantial dishes, popular in each restaurant. Sumptuously gifted as the Gastrodrome chefs are, you don't have to be Escoffier to emulate them. While the dishes may be novel in concept or in presentation, they are simple and easy to cook at home.

The Gastrodrome is the creation of that maverick visionary Sir Terence Conran. Famous for founding Habitat and building up Storehouse plc, Conran has had a love affair with restaurants that dates back to the time he worked as a *plongeur* in Paris in the 1950s. He revels in restaurant minutiae: the sifting of ingredients; the bustle of a working kitchen; the nuances of interior design; the glow of satisfied customers; the glamour of polished cutlery, glasses and fine linen. The Conran portfolio that began with the Soup Kitchen in 1954 now includes Bibendum in the old Michelin tyre factory in Chelsea, Quaglino's in St James's, and Mezzo in Soho.

In fine weather, with tables spilling out on to the riverfront, the Gastrodrome seats 750 customers. The redesigned warehouses look like the set of a culinary epic, with delivery boys rushing to and fro carrying crates of oysters, loaves of bread and boxes of vegetables; with chefs concocting dishes; with customers

hungrily perusing menus or ambling down the cobblestone streets, replete from a hearty meal.

People these days eat with their eyes as much as with their stomachs, so Conran has created a family of restaurants and shops bound as much by a common aesthetic as by their physical proximity. This aesthetic was formed by his own designer's eye. But what is that eye? Conran has always been impressed by the Modernist Movement of the 1920s and 1930s which stressed simplicity and practicality. The design of the Gastrodrome is a practical synthesis of this period's characteristics: industrial finishes are left intact and everything is 'on show', especially the kitchens. The Blue Print Café is virtually neo-Modernist in design.

Modernism was a riposte to the pomp and circumstance of the Victorians and Edwardians who insisted on hiding functionality and applying a veneer of exaggerated gentility over everything. A much-loved symbol of that era is, of course, Tower Bridge (built in 1894) just a few yards from the Gastrodrome. It is the antithesis of Modernism, and Conran can't resist having a joke at its Gothic extravagances. But he knows not to be too iconoclastic about a cherished landmark. 'If you can find a way of doing things that are right for the moment in time, but have a connection with people's good memories of the past,' says Conran, 'then you have something that gives people comfort.'

The Gastrodrome's success has amazed even Conran himself. Perhaps it shouldn't. We have centres of drama, art and music on the South Bank, with more to come at Bankside power station and the Globe Theatre, so why not food? And the name? 'I was mulling it over with a French friend while working on a project in Paris,' muses Conran. '"Trouble is what to call it," I said. "Food complex? Food centre? Our terminology is so awful. What would the French call it?" My friend shrugged, and with a mischievous glint, replied, "A gastrodrome".'

As word of the Gastrodrome got round, Conran was bombarded with proposals to do similar projects. 'I can think of at least half a dozen we have been offered,' he says in early 1995. 'The Bluebird Garage on the King's Road in Chelsea is the only one we are doing – so far.'

Fresh flowers feature prominently, and are chosen to complement the style of the restaurants.

BLUE PRINT CAFÉ

'The simpler the better'
Lucy Crabb

The Blue Print Café is the most established restaurant in the Gastrodrome. It opened in 1989 on the first floor of the Design Museum 100 yards downstream of the Butlers Wharf Building. Of all the Gastrodrome restaurants it has the best views of Docklands, Tower Bridge and the City.

Conran had originally intended it to serve as a café for the design firms and architectural practices that he had hoped to lure to Butlers Wharf. But as soon as the Blue Print Café opened, pinstripes considerably outnumbered loose-fitting suits and ponytails, a ratio which, in the absence of many architectural practices and design firms at Butlers Wharf, has not significantly changed. The name Blue Print comes from the design magazine whose first six issues were backed by Conran and Ruth (now Lady) Rogers.

Swiftly built and costing some £200,000, the interior of the Blue Print Café looks vaguely like a yacht in the Modernist style: glass brick partitions; polished oak floor; simple Formica tables; non-slip rubber table mats; Odeon black cutlery by David Mellor; utilitarian stainless steel bar counter; columns rounded off and fitted out as waiters' stations; a giant porthole looking into the kitchen and bright marine light that floods in off the Thames rinsing the room. Even the gleaming stainless steel litter bin and fire extinguisher add lustre to the interior. With the ice machine clanking away behind the bar, the low ceiling and the vast expanse of water below, you could almost be on the bridge of a yacht. At either end of the Café, wall-mirrors reflect Tower Bridge, the City and Docklands, so that even if you're sitting well away from the windows you can still see the view. Outside there is a balcony covered by a large yellow awning for use in summer.

Conran knew very clearly what sort of food he wanted at Blue Print – light, fresh, simple modern food of the type that was fashionable on the west coast of the USA and in Australia and that suited the style of the room, the price level

Opposite: Weather permitting, the Blue Print Café – like all the Gastrodrome restaurants – provides an opportunity for eating al fresco. Graphic simplicity is the order of the day for table settings.

The restaurant interior is simple and uncluttered. Large, gleaming columns are fitted out as waiter stations, with shelves for cutlery and condiments.

and market. Ever since the first (American) chef departed, the cooking
has inched eastwards and northwards towards England.

The chef, Lucy Crabb, was born in Devon in 1965 and raised in
Wales, a few hundred yards from the Walnut Tree Inn in Abergavenny,
where she helped out in the holidays. She applied for, and got, a job
working for Simon Hopkinson at Bibendum which, she says, 'was bril-
liant. I learnt everything from Simon. He makes you think for yourself
about food. He encourages you to go out and eat. He pushes you but in
a gentle way. He teaches very high standards of organization, cleanliness and speed.' After two and a half years, she left for Kensington
Place restaurant in Notting Hill Gate: 'I really liked the restaurant and
the food, but the kitchen was a shell shock. It was so small and manic.'
Lucy then worked as a pastry chef for Bryan Webb at Hilaire restaurant
in South Kensington before being plucked to the Blue Print Café.

The cooking at the Blue Print Café defies easy categorization: its modern
British that eschews traditional ingredients, adding Mediterranean and Oriental
touches to familiar English mainstays. It's been said that the food is the opposite of that of Rod Eggleston at the Butlers Wharf Chop-house: one uses new
ingredients in traditional ways; the other uses traditional ingredients in new
ways. An example of new English cooking, Blue Print Café-style, is Roast
Pheasant Breast with Puy Lentils, Pancetta and Braised Garlic. Most food crit-
ics call it 'eclectic'. It's got a bit of everything in it: Thai, French, English. 'I
quite like plain food,' says Lucy, 'not played around with. The simpler the
better. If you buy really good ingredients and you don't play around with them,
you'll cook something that's tasty and enjoyable. There's no need to smother
things in heavy sauces.'

The Blue Print Café's dishes use inexpensive ingredients that you can buy in
supermarkets and delicatessens. 'You may be better off buying pak-choi [see

Timbale of Prawns and Lemongrass Wrapped in Pak-choi, page 24] and chillies in an Oriental supermarket. To obtain hake and John Dory, you may have to go to a fishmonger, who can fillet them for you.

'Roast Leeks and Peppers with Shaved Parmesan is such a simple starter, but it's so tasty because it doesn't take anything away from the vegetables. Baked Salmon with a Horseradish Crust perks up what is these days a very ordinary fish and makes it look glamorous. Although I love Oriental food, Hot Spiced Mussels with Coconut and Coriander is an Indian dish that's spicy and easy to cook. Roast Hake is an under-used fish; I cook it with saffron, capers and tomato sauce. Pappardelle with Butternut Squash, Rocket and Parmesan makes a delicious summer dish. But my favourite is Apple and Calvados Parfaît with Hot Apple Fritters and Stewed Blackberry Compôte which is a marriage of frozen parfaît with hot compôte.'

Photographs from the architectural and design magazine, *Blue Print*, adorn one wall, which is punctuated by a large porthole window through to the kitchen. Elegant bentwood beech chairs, designed by Thonet, have become a classic of the Modernist movement.

BLUE PRINT CAFÉ

STARTERS
Roast Leeks and Peppers with Shaved Parmesan
Lentil and Feta Salad with Lemon and Mint Dressing
Hot Spiced Mussels with Coconut and Coriander
Sweet Pickled Herring with Beetroot, Horseradish and Crème Fraîche
Timbale of Prawns and Lemongrass Wrapped in Pak-Choi
Rabbit Terrine with Apple Jelly

MAIN COURSES
Pappardelle with Butternut Squash, Rocket and Parmesan
Roast Hake with Saffron, Caper and Tomato Sauce
Baked Salmon with a Horseradish Crust and Tomato Sauce
Rare Grilled Tuna with Tomato Salsa and Guacamole
John Dory with Black Bean and Ginger Sauce
Roast Chicken Breast with Seed Mustard and Tarragon Sauce
Roast Duck with Plum Sauce
Roast Pheasant Breast with Puy Lentils, Pancetta and Braised Garlic

DESSERTS
Pink Grapefruit Sorbet
Apple and Calvados Parfait with Hot Apple Fritters and Blackberry
Compôte
Orange and Almond Cake with Eugenies
Mascarpone Cheesecake with Bananas and Hot Butterscotch Sauce
Walnut Tart
Hot Chocolate Soufflés

ROAST LEEKS AND PEPPERS WITH SHAVED PARMESAN ✪

Serves 4

6 slender leeks, cut in half diagonally
3 red peppers, cut in half
150 ml / 5 fl oz / ⅔ cup olive oil
Salt and freshly ground black pepper
65 ml / 2½ fl oz / ⅓ cup white wine
1–2 tbsp tarragon, coarsely chopped
100 g / 4 oz piece Parmesan cheese

Pre-heat the oven to 200°C/400°F/gas mark 6.

Wash the leeks well in plenty of cold running water. Bring a large pan of water to the boil and blanch the leeks for about 1 minute. Drain. Do not refresh.

Put the peppers on an oven tray and cook in the oven until the skin is completely black. Remove, place in a bowl and cover with clingfilm (this will help the skins to come off). When the peppers have cooled a little, remove the skins and seeds, and cut into thick strips.

Put half the olive oil, and the salt and pepper in a roasting pan and place in the oven until smoking. Add the blanched leeks and roast until nicely browned.

Remove the roasting pan from the oven and sprinkle the leeks with white wine, then remove them from the pan. Combine all the pan juices, the tarragon and the remaining olive oil to make a dressing. Season to taste.

To serve, place three pieces of leek in the centre of each plate, and arrange six strips of pepper in a criss-cross pattern around the outside. Spoon over some of the dressing. Use a potato peeler to shave long strips of Parmesan, and place these on top of the leeks. Serve warm.

LENTIL AND FETA SALAD WITH LEMON AND MINT DRESSING ✪

Serves 4

1 small onion, finely chopped
1 small carrot, very finely chopped
1 stick celery, very finely chopped
½ leek, very finely chopped
50 g / 2 oz / ¼ cup butter
100–175 g / 4–6 oz / ½–¾ cup puy lentils
1 bay leaf
4 sprigs thyme
Salt and freshly ground black pepper
2 lemons, zest and juice
6–7 tbsp good-quality olive oil
1 pinch paprika
75 g / 3 oz mixed salad leaves
225 g / 8 oz / 2 cups feta cheese, coarsely grated
50 g / 2 oz red pepper, thinly sliced
4 stems fresh mint, leaves removed

In a sauté pan, sweat the onion, carrot, celery and leek in the butter, but do not allow them to colour. When transparent, add the lentils and stir, pour on enough water to cover, and bring to the boil. Turn the heat down, add the bay leaf and thyme and season. Cook until the water has evaporated and the lentils are cooked. You may need to add more water. Remove the thyme and bay leaf.

When cool, add the lemon zest and juice, olive oil and paprika. Season and chill.

Place a pile of salad leaves in the centre of each plate, place the lentils on top and sprinkle with the grated feta. Decorate with the red pepper. Cut the mint leaves into thin strips and sprinkle over the finished dish.

HOT SPICED MUSSELS WITH COCONUT AND CORIANDER

Serves 4

5 cloves garlic
2.5 cm / 1 in piece of fresh ginger, peeled and chopped
275 ml / 9 fl oz / 1 cup water
½ tbsp vegetable oil
150 g / 5 oz / 1 cup onion, chopped
½ tsp turmeric
½ tsp cumin
2 hot green chillies, finely chopped
½ block creamed coconut, grated
20–30 mussels per person, freshly cleaned
1½ tsp fresh coriander, chopped

Place the garlic, ginger and half the water in a food processor and process until smooth.

In a saucepan, heat the vegetable oil, add the onion and cook until transparent. Add the turmeric, cumin and chillies and cook for a few minutes so that the spices are not powdery.

Add the garlic and ginger mixture and the remaining water and bring to the boil, then reduce the heat and simmer until thick. Add the creamed coconut and allow it to dissolve. Liquidize and pass through a sieve.

Place the mussels in a large saucepan and add the coconut mixture. Seal with a tight-fitting lid and cook at a high heat, giving a few shakes now and then. Cook for about 6 minutes, or until the mussels have all opened. Discard any mussels that remain closed.

Garnish with coriander and serve in bowls.

Hot Spiced Mussels with Coconut and Coriander

SWEET PICKLED HERRING WITH BEETROOT, HORSERADISH AND CRÈME FRAÎCHE

Serves 4

450 g / 1 lb raw beetroot, peeled and diced
2 tbsp horseradish, freshly grated
1 tbsp creamed horseradish
75 g / 3 oz puisse épinard (baby spinach)
Salad dressing, to taste
8 sweet pickled herrings
4 tsp crème fraîche
Small bunch of chives, finely sliced

Put the beetroot in boiling water and simmer until tender. Drain and allow to cool, then place in a food processor and process to a pulp. Add the grated and creamed horseradish, season to taste and chill.

Dress the puisse épinard and divide among the plates. Arrange two herrings on top, place a spoonful of beetroot in the centre, then add a spoonful of crème fraîche on the side and sprinkle with chives. (Red onions, thinly sliced and dribbled with lemon juice, are a good alternative if no chives are available.)

TIMBALE OF PRAWNS AND LEMONGRASS WRAPPED IN PAK-CHOI

Serves 4

4–6 heads pak-choi (Chinese greens)
2 tbsp sesame oil
1 stick lemongrass, very finely chopped
5 shallots, finely sliced
2.5 cm / 1 in piece fresh ginger, finely chopped
2 cloves garlic
2 small red chillies, finely chopped
1 lime, juiced
4 tsp soy sauce
Salt and freshly ground black pepper
1 bunch spring onions, thinly sliced on the diagonal
1¹/₂ tbsp sesame seeds, toasted
450 g / 1 lb cooked prawns, in brine or fresh
Coriander, chopped, to taste

Finely slice the base of the pak-choi as far as the leaves, wash the stems and leaves well and keep to one side.

Heat the sesame oil until hot. Add the lemongrass, shallots, ginger, garlic and chillies and fry quickly over a high heat. Throw in the sliced pak-choi stems and cook until just soft, but still slightly crunchy. Remove from the heat and add the lime juice, soy sauce, salt and pepper. Allow to cool. When completely cold, add the prawns and coriander.

In a pan of boiling water, blanch the pak-choi leaves for 10 seconds, then refresh under cold running water. Drain and dry.

Take four moulds or ramekins and brush the insides with sesame oil. Line with the blanched pak-choi leaves with the outside of the leaf facing inwards. Pack the prawn mixture tightly into the moulds with plenty of the juice. Cover with more pak-choi leaves, wrap with clingfilm and put a plate with a heavy weight on top to squeeze out any extra juice. Chill overnight. Reserve any juices and mix with a little sesame oil and soy sauce to make a dressing.

Turn the timbales out on to the centre of each plate. Garnish with spring onions and sesame seeds, dribble dressing over and serve.

RABBIT TERRINE WITH APPLE JELLY

Serves 6–8

Terrine
1 rabbit, skinned and cleaned
150 g / 6 oz pancetta, diced
225 g / 8 oz streaky bacon
4 tbsp olive oil
75 g / 3 oz / ²/₃ cup shallots, finely chopped
2 cloves garlic, finely chopped
2–3 tbsp mixed chopped herbs: sage, parsley, chervil and
  tarragon
100 g / 4 oz / 1 cup pistachios
1¹/₂ tbsp green peppercorns
4 tbsp Cognac
65 ml / 2¹/₂ fl oz / ¹/₄ cup white wine
Salt and freshly ground black pepper

Apple Jelly
Makes about 4 litres / 7 pints / 11¹/₂ cups
3.5 kg / 8 lb Bramley cooking apples
1.75 kg / 4 lb / 8 cups granulated sugar

Please note: the rabbit terrine takes 3 days to prepare.

Terrine

Remove all the meat from the rabbit, keeping the loins whole (the loins are the part of the body between the rib cage and the hip bones). Place the meat from the legs and the diced pancetta into a mincer and mince finely. Wrap the streaky bacon around the loins.

In a heavy pan, heat the olive oil and sweat the shallots and garlic until transparent. Add the herbs, remove from the heat and cool. In a bowl, mix together the minced meat, cold shallots, pistachios and green peppercorns, and season. Pour the Cognac and white wine over and season. Gently place the loins on top and wrap in clingfilm. Marinate for 48 hours, stirring occasionally.

Pre-heat the oven to 160°C/325°F/gas mark 3.

Unwrap the streaky bacon from the loins and line a terrine mould with it. Cook a little of the minced meat mixture in a frying pan to check the flavour, as you may need more herbs or seasoning. Then put half the filling in the bottom of the mould, make a channel down the centre with the side of your hand and place the loins down the centre (which will keep them from moving). Put in the rest of the filling and press down evenly. Fold the bacon over the top and cover with a strip of baking parchment and foil. Cook in a bain-marie in the centre of the oven for 1–1¹/₂ hours.

Remove the terrine from the bain-marie, put a weight on top and refrigerate until set.

Peel off the cling film and cut the terrine across into 15 mm/³/₄ in slices and serve with the apple jelly. This recipe also works well with chicken.

Apple Jelly

Coarsely chop the apples (do not peel or core). Place in a very large saucepan and just cover with water. Bring to the boil and then cook at a gentle simmer. Reduce to about two-thirds, which will take 4–5 hours. When reduced, strain overnight, using a jelly bag.

Next day, measure the juice and for each pint of liquid, add 450 g/1 lb/2 cups of sugar.

Place the sugar and liquid in a saucepan. Skim off any impurities. Bring to the boil and boil hard for 15–30 minutes until setting point is reached. Test this by pouring a little of the liquid on to a cold saucer, then run your finger over the top of the jelly. If it wrinkles, setting point has been reached. Cool slightly and pour into hot, sterilized jars. Cover. Once these are completely cold, the jars can be stored in the refrigerator.

To make mint apple jelly, add two to three tablespoons of freshly chopped mint. Tarragon is also a good herb to flavour the jelly.

Serve with the cold terrine and hot meat dishes.

BLUE
PRINT
CAFÉ

PAPPARDELLE WITH BUTTERNUT SQUASH, ROCKET AND PARMESAN Ⓥ

Serves 4

2 butternut squash
Olive oil
50 g / 2 oz / 1¼ cup butter
1 pinch nutmeg
Sea salt and freshly ground black pepper
600 ml / 1 pint / 2½ cups double (heavy) cream
100 g / 4 oz / 1 cup Parmesan cheese, freshly grated
450 g / 1 lb fresh pappardelle (or tagliatelle)
100 g / 4 oz rocket

Pre-heat the oven to 190°C/375°F/gas mark 5.

Peel the squash, remove the seeds and set aside. Cut the flesh into large chunks.

Wash and dry the seeds, and place on a roasting tray. Sprinkle with sea salt and dribble with olive oil. Toast until golden brown, then allow to cool.

In a large frying pan, melt the butter and add the squash. Cook until soft but not mushy. Season with a generous pinch of nutmeg, salt and a little black pepper. Drain the squash and keep on one side.

Put the cream and a quarter of the cheese into a frying pan and reduce by half.

Meanwhile, cook the pasta in salted boiling water for about 2 minutes or until it is just tender but still firm (*al dente*). Drain and put into a large bowl.

Add the squash to the cream and cheese sauce and heat through.

Add the rocket to the sauce (the rocket should wilt, not cook, so only add it at the very last minute.) Pour the sauce over the pasta, and mix them together. Sprinkle with the remaining Parmesan and the toasted squash seeds.

ROAST HAKE WITH SAFFRON, CAPER AND TOMATO SAUCE

Serves 4

1 pinch saffron
175 ml / 6 fl oz / ¾ cup fish stock (see page 136)
350 g / 12 oz / 1½ cups unsalted butter
4 tbsp olive oil
4 x 175 g / 6 oz hake steaks, skins left on
100 g / 3 oz / ½ cup flour, seasoned
4 large plum tomatoes, peeled and cut into small dice
3 tbsp extra-fine capers
3 tbsp chives, finely chopped
275 g / 10 oz puisse épinard (baby spinach), picked and dried
Salt and freshly ground black pepper

Pre-heat the oven to 230°C/450°F/gas mark 8.

In a large saucepan, add the saffron to the fish stock and bring to the boil. Coarsely dice the butter and gradually whisk it into the boiling stock, one piece at a time. When all the butter is incorporated, remove the sauce from the heat and keep warm.

Pour the olive oil into a roasting tin and heat in the oven until smoking.

Dust the hake with seasoned flour and place in the smoking oil. Roll it over to coat it with oil. Roast in the oven for 12 minutes, or until firm and golden.

Bring the sauce back to the boil and add the tomatoes, capers and two tablespoons of the chives. Stir and check the seasoning.

Place a pile of puisse épinard on each plate, put a piece of hake on top and pour the sauce over. Garnish with the remaining chives and serve the extra sauce separately.

BLUE
PRINT
CAFÉ

MAIN COURSES

BAKED SALMON WITH A HORSERADISH CRUST AND TOMATO SAUCE

Serves 4

Horseradish Crust
175 g / 6 oz / 3/4 cup unsalted butter
75 g / 3 oz smoked salmon, finely chopped
100 g / 4 oz / 1/2 cup horseradish, freshly grated
75 g / 3 oz / 1/3 cup smooth Dijon mustard
1 tbsp creamed horseradish
1 bunch spring onions, finely sliced
200 g / 7 oz / 3 1/2 cups fine cooked breadcrumbs
1 egg, beaten
Splash of Tabasco sauce

Tomato Sauce
1 onion, finely chopped
3 tbsp olive oil
1 garlic clove, crushed
1 large sprig fresh basil, to taste
450 g / 1 lb / 2 cups plum tomatoes, tinned and peeled
1 tsp sugar
Salt and freshly ground black pepper

Baked Salmon
4 x 100–175 g / 4–6 oz salmon fillets, skinned
Salt and freshly ground black pepper
10 chives, finely chopped

Horseradish Crust
In a bowl, beat the butter until just pale and soft, then add all the other ingredients. Keep in a cool place.

Tomato Sauce
In a heavy pan sauté the onion in the olive oil until transparent. Add the garlic and basil, and stir. Add the tomatoes and a little sugar and simmer until thick. Remove from the heat and cool slightly. Liquidize in a blender or food processor, and pass through a fine sieve. Check the seasoning.

Baked Salmon
Pre-heat the oven to 220°C/425°F/gas mark 7.

Season the four salmon fillets, then place in an oven-proof dish and firmly pack the crust on to the top of each. With a knife make diagonal lines across the crust for an attractive appearance. Place in the hot oven until the crust is golden-brown and the salmon is cooked (about 10–15 minutes).

Serve the salmon on the sauce and garnish it with chives.

RARE GRILLED TUNA WITH TOMATO SALSA AND GUACAMOLE

Serves 4

Salsa
6 tomatoes, skinned, seeded and finely diced (concassé)
4 small red chillies, finely diced
1 clove garlic, mashed
1 medium red onion, finely chopped
1 tbsp coriander, finely chopped
2 limes, juiced
Salt and freshly ground black pepper

Guacamole
2 ripe avocados
1 clove garlic
2 limes (1 juiced, 1 cut into quarters)
1 onion
Salt and freshly ground black pepper
1 tbsp crème fraîche

Tuna
4 x 100–175 g / 4–6 oz tuna steaks
Salt and freshly ground black pepper
4 tbsp olive oil

Salsa

Mix all the ingredients together in a bowl. Season to taste. Keep on one side.

Guacamole

Put the avocados into a blender with the garlic and the juice of one lime. Grate the onion and add only the juice to the avocado mixture. Blend the mixture until smooth. Check the seasoning and stir in the crème fraîche. Keep on one side.

Tuna

Heat a grill (broiler) or frying pan until hot. Season the tuna and brush with olive oil. Cook the steaks for 2 minutes on each side. They are best served rare, but can be cooked for longer. Be careful that they are not too dry.

Serve the steaks with the salsa and guacamole on the side. Sprinkle with coriander and dribble with olive oil. Garnish with lime quarters.

MAIN COURSES

JOHN DORY WITH BLACK BEAN AND GINGER SAUCE

Serves 4

5 cm / 2 in piece fresh ginger, peeled
2 tbsp sesame oil
1 clove garlic, very finely sliced
1 small red chilli, very finely chopped
1 large shallot, sliced
1 stick lemongrass, finely chopped
250 ml / 8 fl oz / 1 cup fish stock (see page 136)
2 x 4 oz / 120 g tins Chinese fermented black beans
2 tsp arrowroot
2 fresh lime leaves
4 x 175–225 g / 6–8 oz John Dory fillets, skinned
Salt and freshly ground black pepper
1 tbsp coriander, chopped

Cut the ginger into fine, thin pieces.

Heat the sesame oil in a large saucepan and sweat the ginger, garlic, chilli, shallot and lemongrass. When cooked, add the fish stock and reduce by half.

Meanwhile, put a pan of water on to boil. Tip the black beans into the boiling water, remove from the heat and drain (this is just to take some of the saltiness away.) Add the beans to the mixture in the saucepan and bring to the boil.

Mix the arrowroot with a little water to dissolve it. When smooth, add to the bean mixture. You want the sauce to have a nice coating consistency. Season. Cut the lime leaves into fine thin strips, and add to the mixture. Keep warm.

Season the tuna fillets and steam for 8–10 minutes, or until cooked.

Place a fillet on each plate and spoon the sauce around. Garnish with the coriander.

ROAST CHICKEN BREAST WITH SEED MUSTARD AND TARRAGON SAUCE

Serves 4

Olive oil
4 x 175–225 g / 6–8 oz corn-fed chicken breasts, skin removed
Salt and freshly ground black pepper
1 tbsp butter
2 garlic cloves, smashed
2 shallots, finely sliced
1 small bunch thyme
1 bay leaf
120 ml / 4 fl oz / 1/2 cup white wine
450 ml / 15 fl oz / 2 cups dark chicken stock (see page 136)
1–2 tbsp fresh tarragon, chopped, stalks reserved
450 ml / 15 fl oz / 2 cups double (heavy) cream
1–2 tbsp coarse-grain mustard
Butter

Pre-heat the oven to 200°C/400°F/gas mark 6.

Pour a little olive oil into a roasting pan, add the chicken breasts and season. Cook in the pre-heated oven for 15–20 minutes, or until roasted.

Meanwhile, melt the butter in a saucepan, then add the garlic, shallots, thyme and bay leaf and cook until the shallots are transparent. Pour the white wine over the ingredients and reduce by half. Add the chicken stock and reserved tarragon stalks and reduce by half again. Add the double cream and reduce by half again. Strain the sauce through a sieve then pour it back into the saucepan and keep warm.

Add the mustard and tarragon leaves to the sauce and check the seasoning. Whisk in a little cold butter.

Place the chicken breasts on individual plates and pour the sauce over.

Tuna

Nibbles Shrimp

Shrimp —

Tuna — Fish Cas

Salmon — Poached

Hollandaise.

MAIN COURSES

ROAST DUCK WITH PLUM SAUCE

Serves 4

50 g / 2 oz / ¹/₃ cup shallots, finely chopped
3 tbsp olive oil
100 g / 4 oz blackcurrants, stems removed
1 tbsp runny honey
450 g / 1 lb plums, pitted and quartered
1 tbsp green peppercorns
Splash of cassis (optional)
Salt and freshly ground black pepper
1 bunch watercress
4 x 175 g / 6 oz duck breasts, skin left on

Pre-heat the oven to 230°C/450°F/gas mark 8.

   Put the shallots into a frying pan and sweat in the olive oil until transparent. Add the blackcurrants and honey and cook for 1–2 minutes. Add the plum pieces and cook until soft, but keep the plums' shape: you do not want mush. Add the peppercorns and the cassis (if desired). Season with salt and pepper.

   Score the skin on the duck breasts and season them all over. Place in a roasting tin and cook for 10–15 minutes, depending on how pink you prefer them.

   Serve the breasts with a watercress garnish and a little sauce, with the remaining sauce on the side.

ROAST PHEASANT BREAST WITH PUY LENTILS, PANCETTA AND BRAISED GARLIC

Serves 4

2 garlic heads
175 g / 6 oz pancetta, cut into strips
1 medium onion, finely chopped
1 large carrot, finely chopped
2 sticks celery, finely chopped
1 leek, finely chopped
450 g / 1 lb / 2 cups puy lentils, washed
1 tbsp thyme, to taste
1 bay leaf
1.2 litres / 2 pints / 5 cups chicken stock (see page 136)
3 tbsp olive oil
4 pheasant breasts
2 tbsp parsley, chopped

Pre-heat the oven to 200°C/400°F/gas mark 6.

   Remove all the cloves from the garlic and peel. Chop one clove for the lentils, and reserve the rest.

   In a large saucepan, brown the pancetta. When cooked, add the chopped garlic, onion, carrot, celery and leek, and sweat them in the fat until transparent. Add the lentils, thyme and bay leaf and cover with the chicken stock. Cook until the lentils are tender.

   In a large frying pan, brown the garlic cloves in the olive oil. Transfer them into a roasting tin, cover with chicken stock and season. Place in the middle of the oven to braise.

   Season the pheasant breasts, place in a roasting tin and roast for 10–15 minutes. Rest for 5 minutes.

   To serve, place a mound of lentils in the middle of each plate. Arrange a pheasant breast on top, scatter with the braised garlic, and garnish with parsley.

PINK GRAPEFRUIT SORBET

Serves 4

250 ml / 8 fl oz / 1 cup water
250 ml / 8 fl oz / 1 cup dry white wine
275 g / 10 oz / 1¼ cups caster sugar
500 ml / 17 fl oz / 2 cups pink grapefruit juice
1 measure Campari or grenadine (optional)

Put the water, white wine and sugar in a saucepan and bring to the boil to dissolve the sugar.

Remove from the heat, allow to cool then chill in the refrigerator. Add the grapefruit juice, and Campari for extra colour.

Churn in an ice-cream machine, following the manufacturer's instructions.

APPLE AND CALVADOS PARFAÎT WITH HOT APPLE FRITTERS AND BLACKBERRY COMPÔTE

Serves 4

Parfaît
4 Golden Delicious apples
100 g / 4 oz / ½ cup caster sugar
150 ml / 5 fl oz / ⅔ cup white wine
½ cinnamon stick
½ vanilla pod
1 clove
3 tbsp Calvados
3 egg yolks
150 ml / 5 fl oz / ½ cup double (heavy) cream

Apple Fritters
90 g / 3½ oz / ⅔ cup plain flour
1 pinch salt

½ tbsp olive oil
1½ tbsp white wine
65 ml / 2½ fl oz / ¼ cup water
2 tbsp caster sugar
1 tsp cinnamon
2 egg whites
3 Golden Delicious apples
1.2 litres / 2 pints / 5 cups vegetable oil
Flour for dusting

Blackberry Compôte
1 kg / 2 lb / 7 cups blackberries
50 g / 2 oz / ¼ cup caster sugar
65 ml / 2½ fl oz / ¼ cup water

Parfaît
Peel, core and slice the apples.

In a thick-bottomed saucepan, put half the sugar, the apples, white wine, cinnamon, vanilla and clove, then gently cook until thick, and most of the liquid has evaporated. Remove the spices. Liquidize the apple mixture in a blender or food processor and pass through a sieve. Add the Calvados, allow to cool and then chill in the refrigerator.

Beat the egg yolks and remaining sugar together until pale and thick and doubled in volume. Whip the double cream to soft peaks. Fold the apple purée into the egg mixture, then add the whipped cream.

Pour into a 450 g / 1 lb loaf tin, lined with clingfilm, and freeze overnight.

Apple Fritters
In a mixing bowl, sift the flour and salt together. Make a well in the centre and mix in the olive oil and white wine. Gradually beat in the water, until you have a thick batter. You may not need all the water. Put aside for 1 hour.

Mix together the cinnamon and caster sugar.

Beat the egg whites until stiff and fold into the batter.

Apple and Calvados Parfaît with Hot Apple Fritters and Blackberry Compôte

Peel and core the apples, and slice in 5 mm/¹/₄ in rings. Heat the oil in a large saucepan. Dust the apple rings with flour, dip into the batter and fry at 190°C/375°F until golden. Drain on kitchen paper, and keep warm.

To serve, roll each fritter in the cinnamon and caster sugar.

Blackberry Compôte

Put the blackberries, sugar and water into a saucepan and stew until soft, but not completely mushy. Check the sweetness and serve.

Serve two thin slices of parfaît on each plate with three apple fritters and a generous serving of compôte.

ORANGE AND ALMOND CAKE WITH EUGENIES

Serves 4

Cake
3 eggs, separated
100 g / 4 oz / 1/2 cup caster sugar
Zest of one orange
65 ml / 2 1/2 fl oz / 1 1/4 cup orange juice
2 drops almond essence
50 g / 2 oz / 1/3 cup plain flour
100 g / 4 oz / 1 cup ground almonds
1 tbsp caster sugar
100 g / 4 oz / 1/2 cup butter, melted

Mascarpone Filling
100 g / 4 oz / 1/2 cup mascarpone cheese
2 tbsp Grand Marnier
1 tbsp orange juice
1/2 split vanilla pod, seeds only
2–3 tbsp icing sugar

Decoration
Cocoa, for dusting
Icing sugar, for dusting
20–30 Eugenies

Eugenies
275 g / 10 oz / 1 1/2 cups caster sugar
150 ml / 5 fl oz / 2/3 cup water
3 oranges
175 g / 6 oz good-quality dark chocolate

Cake
Pre-heat the oven to 180°C/350°F/gas mark 4.

Line two 20 cm/8 in or one 23 cm/9 in sponge (cake) tins with greaseproof paper, butter and dust with flour.

Whisk the egg yolks and sugar until light and fluffy. Mix in the orange zest, orange juice and almond essence. Sift the flour and add it to the mixture with the ground almonds.

Beat the egg whites with the caster sugar until stiff. Stir the melted butter into the almond mixture and then fold the whites in.

Pour into the lined tins and bake until golden and springy. Turn out and cool.

If made in a 23 cm/9 in tin, the cake can simply be dusted with icing sugar and served with tea. Alternatively, sandwich the two layers together with the mascarpone filling, dust with cocoa and pile the Eugenies on top.

Mascarpone Filling
Beat all the ingredients together and chill.

Eugenies
Bring the sugar and water to the boil in a heavy saucepan, then turn down to a gentle simmer to allow the sugar to dissolve.

Peel off long strips of orange peel, without any pith as this makes them very bitter. Put the strips of peel into the syrup and cook gently for about 30 minutes, so that the peel is soft but retains its shape. Remove from the heat and drain on a wire rack.

When the peel is completely cold, melt the chocolate in a double-boiler. Dip the strips of peel in the chocolate, and spread out on silicone paper to set.

The Eugenies can be used as they are, or toss them in cocoa or icing sugar.

DESSERTS

MASCARPONE CHEESECAKE WITH BANANAS AND HOT BUTTERSCOTCH SAUCE

Serves 8

Cheesecake

2 eggs, separated
225 g / 8 oz / 1 cup mascarpone cheese
75 g / 3 oz / 1/3 cup caster sugar
1/2 tsp vanilla essence
1/2 vanilla pod, split lengthways, seeds removed
3 tsp gelatine, dissolved in cold water
250 ml / 8 fl oz / 1 cup double (heavy) cream, lightly whipped
100 g / 4 oz / 1 cup digestive (sweet wheatmeal) biscuits, crushed
65 g / 2 1/2 oz / 1/4 cup butter, melted
2–3 bananas

Butterscotch Sauce

120 ml / 4 fl oz / 1/2 cup double (heavy) cream
75 g / 3 oz / 1/3 cup unsalted butter
150 g / 5 oz / 3/4 cup soft dark brown sugar
1/2 vanilla pod

Cheesecake

In the bowl of an electric mixer, beat together the egg yolks, mascarpone, two-thirds of the sugar, the vanilla essence and vanilla seeds, until light and fluffy. Add the dissolved gelatine, then fold in the cream.

Beat the egg whites to a stiff meringue with the remaining sugar. Then fold the mascarpone mixture into the egg whites.

In a separate bowl, bind the biscuits with the melted butter. Press the biscuits into the base of a 15 cm/6 in springform tin. Pour in the cheesecake mixture, cover and chill overnight in the refrigerator.

Slice the bananas and arrange on top of the

Mascarpone Cheesecake with Bananas and Hot Butterscotch Sauce

cheesecake, and serve the sauce poured over or on the side.

Butterscotch Sauce

Put all the ingredients into a saucepan and bring to the boil. Heat until the sauce is shiny and smooth. Remove the vanilla pod and cool slightly before serving (if you pour it over the cheesecake when it is too hot, the cake will melt).

WALNUT TART

Serves 4

1/2 quantity sweet pastry (see page 142)
100 g / 4 oz / 1/3 cup golden syrup
75 g / 3 oz / 1/3 cup caster sugar
1 1/2 tbsp plain flour, sifted
1/2 tsp salt
2 eggs, beaten
2 tbsp butter, melted
100 g / 4 oz / 1 cup walnuts
Crème fraîche, to serve

Pre-heat the oven to 150°C/300°F/gas mark 2.

Grease a flan ring with butter and dust with flour, then line with the pastry and chill. Line the pastry with greaseproof paper and baking beans. Bake blind for 20–25 minutes until half-cooked. Remove paper and beans.

In a bowl, mix together the syrup and sugar. In a separate bowl, mix the flour and salt with the eggs. Beat the melted butter, syrup and egg mixtures together.

Put a generous layer of walnuts over the bottom of the tart and pour the topping over. Place in the pre-heated oven and cook for 45 minutes – 1 hour or until cooked. The walnuts will rise to the top.

Serve with crème fraîche.

HOT CHOCOLATE SOUFFLÉS

Serves 4

75 g / 3 oz dark chocolate
120 ml / 4 fl oz / 1/2 cup double (heavy) cream
3 eggs, separated
2 tbsp dark rum
1 pinch cream of tartar
2 tbsp caster sugar
Crème fraîche, to serve

Pre-heat the oven to 200°C/400°F/gas mark 6. Prepare four 200 ml/7 fl oz/1 cup ramekins by greasing them with butter and dusting them with caster sugar.

Melt the chocolate and cream together in a saucepan over a gentle heat, then remove and cool slightly.

Whisk the egg yolks and rum into the chocolate. Whisk the egg whites with the cream of tartar, and slowly add the sugar until the mixture is glossy and stiff. Fold the chocolate and egg whites together, then pour into the ramekins. Just before cooking, run a sharp knife around the inside edge of ramekins: this will help the soufflés to rise evenly.

Bake in the top half of the oven for about 10 minutes. Serve immediately with crème fraîche.

This mixture can be made two hours in advance, chilled in the ramekins, and cooked straight from the refrigerator.

'Keep it simple and seasonal'

David Burke

Le Pont de la Tour is the opulent centrepiece of the Gastrodrome and its biggest crowd-puller: summer turnover hits 4,000 covers a week, mid-winter 3,000. Its elegant interior is French- and marine-inspired. Food by David Burke, head chef and shareholder, uses the very best and freshest ingredients, prepared and cooked simply, and served generously.

Sitting in his fourth-floor riverfront offices at Butlers Wharf in early 1991, Conran sketched out in notebooks ideas for Le Pont de la Tour that under Joel Kissin's stewardship would probably seal the fate of Conran's investment in Butlers Wharf once and for all. It would be large enough and good enough to draw customers to the area, with added ramifications: a Bar and Grill, *Salon Privé*, Wine Merchant, Food Store and Bakery, most of which were intended for local residents but whose economic viability was (at least to start with) heavily dependent on the core restaurant itself.

Conran had got a feel for the site and realized that a connection with the river was an important element in the design. Watching boats as they plied the tidal waters of the Thames sparked off the idea of recreating the feel of a dining room in an ocean liner berthed in a dock from which you could peer into passing boats.

By chance, Conran visited the Paris apartment of a friend, Jean-François Bentz, whose family of Nantes shipfitters had worked on the *Normandie* liner. In the hallway Conran's eye alighted on a set of simple upright wood chairs of the same design as those in the second-class dining room of the *Normandie*. 'I liked their look,' he says. 'And I liked the connection with the second-class dining room. First-class had reproduction Louis XV.' Conran measured the chairs and, back in England, designed the 'loose interpretation' in burr-oak that are now in Le Pont de la Tour.

From the riverfront, Le Pont de la Tour looks like a tastefully furnished, elongated aquarium. The rectangular sash windows are lined by fishscale leadwork designed by Patrick Caulfield. Peering through the windows, you can watch the steel-shelled crabs and

Left: The Crustacea Bar acts as a service area to make up seafood dishes for the Bar and Grill.
Right: The bar is panelled with sheets of chequerplate flooring, in the tread of which Conran sees shoals of tiny fish.

Etched with a map of Burgundy, the window of the *Salon Privé* admits light to the room while maintaining a degree of privacy.

lobsters of the modern financial world eating. Caulfield also supplied the design for the etched glass panes (made by Hour Glass) by the main doorway of the restaurant, and the glass partitions in the Bar and Grill. As Caulfield points out: 'The etched glass has a fish-knife design and stylized fish shapes with bubble eyes which have the slight feel of the decor of an ocean liner in the 1930s, like portholes.'

Entering the main doorway, you step across a granite floor whose veining evokes the seabed. To your left stands the Crustacea Bar decked out with lobsters, oysters, langoustines, winkles, crabs and cockles piled up on crushed ice. The crustacea mosaic inlaid into the side of the Bar was inspired by the cover of Alan Davidson's book *Mediterranean Seafood*. Conran commissioned William Bertoia from Friuli to hunt down the originals – Bertoia traced them

A still-life of breads, cheeses, fruit, vegetables and flowers makes a dramatic statement as you walk from the Bar and Grill through to the restaurant.

to the floor of a church in Pompeii – and adapt them. The series continues in the lavatories which are opposite the Crustacea Bar.

After you've paused to admire Tom Dixon's three-metre wire crustacea chandelier hanging above you in the entrance hall, you enter the throng of the Bar and Grill where the food abbreviates that at the restaurant: seafood and French brasserie dishes. The tables in the Bar and Grill are designed by Conran as two pyramids stuck together tip to tip, one pyramid forming the base, the other the table top. The base pyramids are made of riveted zinc, an idea lifted from a building in rue Reamur, Paris, made entirely of rolled-steel joists. They also echo larger rivets in the metal lintels above the ground-floor windows of the Butlers Wharf Building.

Having passed through the Bar and reception area, you finally emerge into

the tranquillity of the restaurant. Dazzling white linen, sea-green carpet, bronzework window frames and cream-painted walls symbolic of 1930s wealth, all are reflected in strategically placed mirrors. 'These materials give a feeling of calm, elegant luxury,' says Conran. 'Bronze – not brass – is important because the colour of bronze gives a feeling of 1930s elegance, whereas brass is 1980s glitz. I appreciate the subtlety of it and I think other people see it as well.'

Caricatures by Sem of early twentieth-century Parisian café society line the walls. Conran bought the complete set from David Batterham, the rare books dealer. Sem, France's answer to Bateman, caricatured Parisian – especially café – society, and Conran deemed his work appropriate for a restaurant with French

overtones so near the City. Most of the restaurant furniture was designed by Conran and produced by Sean Sutcliffe at Benchmark and Paul Litton of Litton Furniture.

The walls at Le Pont de la Tour are low for such an elongated room, so, to create a sense of height, a coffered ceiling was fitted with sunken low-voltage tungsten-halogen spots and a concealed neon light around the pelmet.

Mirrors line both the window frames and the upright pillars running the length of the restaurant, giving kaleidoscopic views of Tower Bridge from almost every table. 'Mirroring is very important in interiors generally, but in restaurants in particular because it creates an added dimension,' says Conran. 'You're never alone with a mirror. It was especially important at Le Pont de la Tour to bring Tower Bridge into the room, so that all sorts of strange views of it should be available to as many people as possible. It's almost impossible to sit in the restaurant and not see some sort of reflection of it.' If for some reason your view is blocked, you can admire the mini-Tower Bridge on the central waiters' station: it's now glued down after the original was stolen.

Above left: Graphics discreetly reinforce the image of the restaurant.
Right: Mirrors play a hugely important role, reflecting and refracting images from inside and out.

The *Salon Privé* seats between ten and twenty people. As in all the restaurants, flowers are changed twice a week.

Paula Pryke, a 35-year-old ex-schoolteacher turned florist, arranges the flowers. '[They] are part of the design,' she says. 'Terence decides where he is going to put the flowers before he has even decided on the fabrics.' Most important is the dramatic display on the piano in the Bar and Grill which enhances the luxuriousness of Le Pont de la Tour. I could save £100,000 a year [at the restaurants] if I didn't have flowers,' observes Conran, 'but they make a real difference.'

At the far end of the restaurant to the right you'll find the entrance to the Wine Merchant which leads on to the *Salon Privé* for parties of between ten and twenty. This has been done up like a cellar with one wall bottle-lined and the others decked with collages that Conran used in his book *Terence Conran's France*. The Wine Merchant provides the wines for Le Pont de la Tour's epic 900-strong blockbuster list (sommeliers take bottles from the shelves as if retrieving wines from a cellar.) Wine consumption at Le Pont de la Tour shatters the myth that the City 'doesn't drink'. Tables of two often work through three bottles, including whole bottles of vintage port. More wine is drunk at lunch than dinner, but the quality is better at dinner.

The atmosphere at Le Pont de la Tour undergoes a transformation between lunch and dinner. Lunch is brasserie-like with a swift *prix fixe* menu. Tables are packed with the Worshipful Company of Arbitrageurs hugger-mugger over deals and gossip, noise levels correlating roughly to market buoyancy. Even the least charismatic 'derivatives' trader can feel glamorous. But lunch is not for wimps: parties often carry on until 5 pm with digestifs and cigars handed round.

At dinner, Le Pont de la Tour metamorphoses into an elegant candle-lit restaurant with à la carte menu and discreet service all set against a backdrop of floodlit Tower Bridge. Most romantic are the window tables at the far end of the room. One young man scrawled in Biro on his tablecloth 'Will you marry

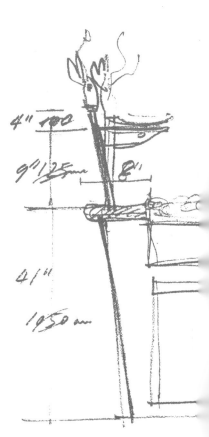

me?' to the girl he was courting. She presumably said 'Yes' because he asked to hang on to the tablecloth, which was added to his bill.

At Le Pont de la Tour, the kitchens are visible as you pass by the reception desk. But there are better views from Shad Thames, where two windows show the back of the kitchens. Here, amid the ballet of white-clad chefs working in a synchronized performance of chopping, slicing, composing, torching and washing, is a slim dark Irishman, David Burke, the head chef. Burke's ascent in the culinary world is remarkable. He is one of nine siblings, and was born in Dublin in 1962. David grew up on Irish staples, like stuffed lambs' hearts and potatoes. Sunday lunch was a piece of bacon with cabbage and heaps of boiled potatoes. He has worked in kitchens since the age of twelve 'to get something to eat', he half-jokes. After catering school in Dublin he worked at Ballymaloe House in Shanagarry, Co. Cork, with Myrtle Allen before training under Simon Hopkinson at Bibendum for two and a half years. Hopkinson recommended him to Conran and Kissin as head chef at Le Pont de la Tour.

His menu mixes regional French, Irish, British and Italian dishes in simple, generous style with no 'messing about', and favours neat, tidy presentation shorn of unnecessary garnishes. Some dishes are the most unashamedly plutocratic and cosmopolitan of all the Gastrodrome restaurants, with such goodies as foie gras, caviare, lobster and sea bass to complement the deep-pile carpet, wine list and army of waiters. Other items are more modest Irish dishes straight out of Burke's childhood, like Champ and Colcannon (see Basic Recipes, pages 139–40) which he has been eating 'since I was two months old. Spuds you can't beat me on.'

The most popular dishes taken from the restaurant menu are: Peppered Ballotine (or Terrine) of Foie Gras; Tomato Mozzarella and Pesto Tart; *Fruits de Mer* with Shallot Vinegar and Mayonnaise; Beef Fillet of Beef with Marrow and Red Wine Sauce; and St Emilion au Chocolat. Conran's favourite is Entrecôte, Frites and Béarnaise.

Sketch by Terence Conran showing side elevation of the Crustacea Bar.

From the street, windows look in to the kitchen, putting the chefs on display and connecting in the minds of passers-by the link between the process of cooking and the pleasures of eating.

LE PONT DE LA TOUR

STARTERS
Parsley Soup
Scrambled Egg with Truffles
Wild Mushrooms on Brioche Toast
Crab and Saffron Tart
Crêpe Parmentier with Smoked Salmon, Caviare and Crème Fraîche
Tomato, Mozzarella and Pesto Tart
Sauté of Scallops with Gremolata
Peppered Ballotine of Foie Gras with Brioche Toast

MAIN COURSES
Plateau de Fruits de Mer with Shallot Vinegar and Mayonnaise
Lobster Pot au Feu
Roast Sea Bass with Olive Oil and Lemon, Served with Champ
Grouse with Bread Sauce
Sauté of Sweetbreads with Morels
Veal Kidneys with Shallots, Pancetta and Thyme
Beef Fillet with Marrow and Red Wine Sauce

DESSERTS
Baked Apple with Sultanas and Calvados
Cinnamon Ice-cream
Walnut and Vieux Prune Ice-cream
St Emilion au Chocolat
Steamed Marmalade Sponge
Chocolate and Hazelnut Tart
Passion Fruit Tart with Crème Fraîche

PARSLEY SOUP

Serves 4

450 g / 1 lb flat-leafed parsley
3 tbsp vegetable oil
275 g / 10 oz / 2 cups onions, finely chopped
275 g / 10 oz / 2 cups leeks, chopped
275 g / 10 oz / 2 cups celery, chopped
2.25 litres / 4 pints / 9 cups chicken stock or good vegetable
*   stock (see page 136)*
300 ml / 10 fl oz / 1¼ cups single (thin) cream
Salt and freshly ground black pepper
Croûtons, to serve (see page 138)

Pick the leaves from the parsley, keeping the stalks on
one side. Chop the leaves coarsely.

In a saucepan, heat the oil and add the onions, leeks,
celery and parsley stalks. Cook over a low heat, until soft.

In a separate saucepan, bring the stock to the boil, add
the vegetable mixture and boil until reduced by half.

Add the chopped parsley and cook for a few minutes,
keeping the leaves green. Remove from the heat and
liquidize in a blender or food processor until smooth.
Pass through a fine sieve and return to the pan.

Gently warm through, then stir in the cream. *Do not
allow to boil.* Adjust seasoning. Serve with croûtons.

SCRAMBLED EGG WITH TRUFFLES ❖

Serves 4

8–12 eggs
50–100 g / 2–4oz truffle
300 ml / 10 fl oz / 1¼ cups double (heavy) cream
100 g / 4oz / ½ cup unsalted butter, at room temperature

Salt and freshly ground black pepper
4 slices brioche (see page 141)

Place the eggs and the truffle in an airtight container
overnight to infuse.

Use two or three eggs per person. Break them into a
large bowl, add half the cream and half the butter, season
and beat with a whisk until fully incorporated. Melt the
remaining butter in a pan, add the eggs and cook until
soft. Add more cream as necessary. Season.

Toast the brioche, and butter it.

Put a slice of brioche toast on each plate, top with
scrambled eggs and shave a generous amount of truffle over.

WILD MUSHROOMS ON BRIOCHE TOAST ❖

Serves 4

1 kg / 2 lb mixed wild mushrooms
75 g / 3 oz / 1½ cup shallots, chopped
3 tbsp olive oil
1 clove garlic, chopped
½ lemon, juiced
½–1 tbsp tarragon, chopped
150 ml / 5 fl oz / ⅔ cup white wine
300 ml / 10 fl oz / 1½ cups double (heavy) cream
Salt and freshly ground black pepper
4 slices brioche, toasted and buttered (see page 141)

Clean the mushrooms and cut into pieces of equal size.

In a saucepan sweat the shallots in the olive oil. Add the
mushrooms and garlic and cook until nearly dry.

Add the lemon juice and tarragon and stir. Add the
white wine and cook for 1–2 minutes. Add the cream, salt
and pepper, and cook until the sauce is thick.

Serve on the brioche.

CRAB AND SAFFRON TART

Serves 4

Pastry
175 g / 6 oz / 1¼ cups plain flour
1 tsp salt
100 g / 4 oz / ½ cup unsalted butter, chilled
1 egg yolk
Iced water, to bind

Custard
175 ml / 6 fl oz / ¾ cup double (heavy) cream
1 large pinch Spanish saffron
1 egg
1 egg yolk

Filling
1 tbsp olive oil
2 shallots, finely chopped
1 clove garlic, finely chopped
5 ripe tomatoes, peeled, seeded and chopped
Salt and freshly ground black pepper
175 g / 6 oz fresh cooked crab meat (ideally fresh, but
  can be tinned or frozen)

Pastry
Pre-heat the oven to 220°C/425°F/gas mark 7.
  In a mixing bowl, combine the flour and salt, and rub in the butter. Mix in the egg yolk and, if necessary, a little water to bind the pastry. Roll out to a thickness of 3 mm/⅛ and line one 20 cm/8 in or four small loose-bottomed tins. Chill for 30 minutes in the refrigerator. Line with greaseproof paper and baking beans. Bake blind for 10 minutes. Remove paper and beans. Reduce the heat to 190°C/375°F/gas mark 5. Bake for another 5–8 minutes, until golden.

Custard
In a heavy pan bring the cream to boiling point then remove from the heat. Add the saffron and infuse for 10–15 minutes.
  In a mixing bowl beat the egg and egg yolk together, then stir in the cream. Keep to one side.

Filling
Pre-heat the oven to 180°C/350°F/gas mark 4.
  Heat the oil in a heavy pan. Cook the shallots until soft, add the garlic and cook for two minutes. Add the tomatoes. Season, and cook very gently until most of the liquid has evaporated and the tomatoes begin to caramelize. Keep to one side.
  Line the pastry tart(s) with a layer of tomato sauce, then cover with cooked crab meat. Season if necessary, then pour custard over the filling. Bake for 20–25 minutes, until set.

STARTERS

Crêpes Parmentier with Smoked Salmon, Caviare and Crème Fraîche

Serves 4

Crêpes
450 g / 1 lb potatoes, peeled and diced
3 tsp plain flour
3 eggs
4 egg whites
50 ml / 2 fl oz / 1/4 cup double (heavy) cream
50 ml / 2 fl oz / 1/4 cup milk
Salt and freshly ground black pepper
Vegetable oil

Topping
100 g / 4 oz smoked salmon
4 tsp crème fraîche
4 tsp Sevruga caviare
1 tbsp chives, chopped
1 lemon, cut into quarters

Crêpes
Pre-heat the oven to 110°C/225°F/gas mark 4.

Put the potatoes in the top of a steamer or double-boiler over simmering water and cook until soft, then mash with the flour. Add the rest of the ingredients, except the oil.

Heat a blini pan (or small frying pan) with a film of vegetable oil across the bottom. When smoking, pour a quarter of the potato mixture into the hot pan. You need to have it about two-thirds full. When nicely brown, flip it over and cook the other side. Place in the oven to keep warm until all four are cooked.

Topping
Place each pancake in the middle of a dinner plate, put smoked salmon in the middle, place a spoonful of crème fraîche on top, then a generous spoonful of caviare. Sprinkle with chives and garnish with the lemon quarters.

Tomato, Mozzarella and Pesto Tart Ⓥ

Serves 4

550 g / 1 lb 4oz puff pastry (see page 141)
3 shallots, chopped
2 tbsp olive oil
1 clove garlic, crushed
5 plum tomatoes, peeled, seeded and chopped
8 leaves basil
225 g / 8 oz buffalo mozzarella cheese, cut into 12 slices
4 tsp pesto (see page 139)
1 egg, beaten
2 tbsp Parmesan cheese
65 ml / 2 1/2 fl oz / 1/3 cup basil oil

Pre-heat the oven to 190°C/375°F/gas mark 5.

Roll out the puff pastry to a thickness of 3 mm/1/8 in, then cut into four circles of 13 cm/5 in diameter. Place on a baking tray lined with silicone paper. Put in the refrigerator for 30 minutes to rest.

Cook the shallots in the olive oil until transparent. Add the garlic and cook for 2 minutes. Add the tomatoes and cook for a further 2 minutes. Add the basil and cook for 1 minute. Remove from the heat. The tomatoes should still be chunky; if the mixture is very wet, strain.

Remove the pastry from the refrigerator and prick all over with a fork. In the centre of each circle place a mound of tomato, leaving a border of about 2.5 cm/1 in all around. Rest three slices of mozzarella against one side of the tomato and top off with the pesto. Brush with egg around the edge.

Place in the top of the oven and bake for 25–30 minutes, until risen and golden. Sprinkle with the Parmesan and dribble with basil oil.

SAUTÉ OF SCALLOPS WITH GREMOLATA

Serves 4

16 fresh scallops
1 clove garlic, finely chopped
Zest of 4 lemons, grated
1 tbsp flat-leafed parsley, chopped
Olive oil or lemon olive oil (such as Colonna Granverde)
Salt and freshly ground black pepper
1 lemon, cut into quarters

Clean and wash the scallops, removing the muscle but leaving the coral.

For the gremolata, put the garlic, lemon zest and parsley in a mixing bowl and combine, then put to one side.

Pour a thick film of olive oil into a saucepan and heat to just below smoking point. Season the scallops. Cook half of them by placing gently in the hot oil and searing quickly on both sides until they acquire a dark crust. Remove from the pan and keep warm. Cook remaining scallops in the same way.

Place four scallops on each plate and sprinkle with gremolata. Drizzle with lemon oil and garnish with lemon wedges.

PEPPERED BALLOTINE OF FOIE GRAS WITH BRIOCHE TOAST

Serves 4

1 lobe (225–450 g / 8 oz–1 lb) foie gras
1 tsp salt
1/2 tsp black pepper
1 pinch nutmeg
2 pinches quatre épices (see page 143)
2 tbsp sherry or port
2 tbsp peppercorns
600 ml / 1 pint / 2 1/2 cups aspic jelly
4 slices brioche, toasted (see page 141)

Remove the membrane and trim the foie gras. Place in a bowl and sprinkle with the salt, pepper, nutmeg, quatre épices and sherry or port.

Marinade in the refrigerator for 24 hours, turning it over after 12 hours.

Fold the foie gras over and shape into a cylinder about 7.5–10 cm/3–4 in in diameter. Wrap very closely with lots of clingfilm tied tightly at each end; it must be watertight. It is better to use too much clingfilm rather than not enough.

Heat a large pan of water to 70–85°C/158–167°F. It is essential that the water does not exceed this temperature. Place the wrapped foie gras in the water. After 12 minutes, remove and plunge into a bowl of water and ice. When completely cold, reshape and put in the refrigerator for a couple of hours.

In a coffee grinder or spice mill, grind the peppercorns, then sieve them to keep the coarser part of the pepper (it should not be too coarse).

Have the aspic just on the point of setting. Unwrap the foie gras and place on a wire rack which has a tray underneath to catch the drips. Spoon the aspic all over the foie gras and place in the refrigerator. When the aspic has set, spoon over another layer and chill. Do this one more time. Sprinkle the third layer of aspic with the coarse pepper, making sure it is covering the top and sides. You do not want it too dense, just well speckled. Chill. Carry on adding aspic and chilling until the foie gras is coated with a layer about 5 mm/1/4 all over.

Slice with a hot knife and serve with toasted brioche.

MAIN COURSES

PLATEAU DE FRUITS DE MER WITH SHALLOT VINEGAR AND MAYONNAISE

Serves 4

Shellfish
2 x 450 g / 1 lb lobsters, cooked
2 x 450 g / 1 lb crabs, cooked
12 langoustines, cooked
12 clams, raw
12 queen scallops, raw
12 oysters, raw
225–450 g / 8 oz–1 lb whelks, cooked
225–450 g / 8 oz–1 lb winkles, cooked
6 lemons, cut into quarters

Accompaniments
2 shallots, very finely chopped
150 ml / 5 fl oz / ⅔ cup good-quality red wine vinegar
300 ml / 10 fl oz / 1¼ cups mayonnaise (see page 137)
Brown bread, freshly baked

Shellfish

Split the lobsters in two lengthways with strong kitchen scissors or shears. Split the crabs in two and remove the 'dead man's fingers'.

On an attractive platter, arrange all the shellfish on a bed of seaweed and crushed ice. Decorate with lemon wedges.

Accompaniments

Make the shallot vinegar by combining the shallots with the vinegar at the last minute.

Serve the platter with the shallot vinegar, mayonnaise, and brown bread. Don't forget to provide finger bowls.

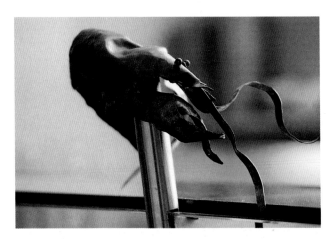

LOBSTER POT AU FEU

Serves 4

Lobster Bisque

4 x 450–750 g / 1–1¹/₂ lb lobsters, cooked
1 bay leaf
1 sprig thyme
4 sprigs parsley
4–6 tbsp olive oil, for browning
120 ml / 4 fl oz / ¹/₂ cup Armagnac
2 carrots, finely chopped
1 onion, finely chopped
1 large celery stick, finely chopped
1 clove garlic, finely chopped
200 ml / 7 fl oz / ³/₄ cup dry white wine
1 pinch of sugar
5 tomatoes, skinned, seeded and chopped
1.2 litres / 2 pints / 5 cups water
Salt and freshly ground black pepper
¹/₂ tsp cayenne pepper
150 ml / 5 fl oz / ²/₃ cup crème fraîche
4 sprigs fresh tarragon, leaves removed

Vegetable Garnish

250 g / 9 oz thin green beans, trimmed
250 g / 9 oz baby onions, peeled
275 g / 10 oz baby courgettes (zucchini), cut in half
    lengthways
200 g / 7 oz cherry tomatoes, halved
4 sprigs fresh chervil

Cut the lobster in half lengthways with strong kitchen scissors or shears. Carefully remove the meat from the body and claws. Keep the shells on one side.

Make a bouquet garni with the bay leaf, thyme and parsley, tied together with string.

Lightly sauté the lobster shells and brown in a little olive oil in a large saucepan. Add the Armagnac and set alight. When the spirit has burned off, add the carrot, onion, celery, garlic, white wine and pinch of sugar. Bring to the boil and add the tomatoes, water, bouquet garni, salt, pepper and cayenne. Simmer for 30 minutes. Strain the liquid and keep hot.

Slice the meat from the lobster and keep the claws whole.

Cook the beans, onions and courgettes separately in boiling water until just cooked. Refresh with cold water.

Stir the crème fraîche and tarragon into the bisque, and check the seasoning.

Put the lobster meat in four large soup plates, add the vegetables and cherry tomatoes and arrange attractively. Pour the hot bisque over the lobster and vegetables, and garnish with the chervil.

ROAST SEA BASS WITH OLIVE OIL AND LEMON, SERVED WITH CHAMP

Serves 4

600 g / 1¹/₄ lb fillet of sea bass, with skin on but scales
    removed
Salt and freshly ground black pepper
150 ml / 5 fl oz / ²/₃ cup extra-virgin olive oil
1 lemon, cut into quarters
1 bunch watercress
1 quantity champ (see page 139)

Score the sea bass on the skin side to prevent curling, and season well. Divide the fish into two to four pieces, depending on the size of your pan.

Heat a thin film of oil in a saucepan to just below smoking point and place the fish skinside down in the pan until a crust forms. Turn over and cook until nicely browned.

Arrange on a serving dish, drizzle the remaining olive oil over and garnish with lemon wedges and fresh watercress.

Serve with champ.

GROUSE WITH BREAD SAUCE

Serves 4

Bread sauce
1.2 litres / 2 pints / 5 cups milk
1 medium onion, stuck with 6 cloves
2 bay leaves
1 tbsp parsley stalks
2 pinches nutmeg, freshly grated
Salt and freshly ground black pepper
100–175 g / 4–6 oz / 2–3 cups fresh breadcrumbs

Gravy
1 small onion, chopped
1 small carrot, chopped
1 small leek, chopped
1 large celery stick, chopped
2 tbsp olive oil
Grouse giblets, wishbones and trimmings
65 ml / 2½ fl oz / ¼ cup Madeira
65 ml / 2½ fl oz / ¼ cup port
1.2 litres / 2 pints / 5 cups water
2 bay leaves
1 tbsp parsley stalks
Salt and freshly ground black pepper

Grouse
4 grouse, wishbone removed
4 tbsp olive oil, for frying
Salt and freshly ground black pepper

Bread Sauce
Start the bread sauce a day before the grouse. Put the milk in a saucepan and add the onion, bay leaves, parsley stalks, nutmeg, a little salt and pepper and infuse over a gentle heat for 30 minutes. Strain and cool, then refrigerate overnight.

The following day, warm the milk and add two-thirds of the breadcrumbs. Check the seasoning and add more grated nutmeg if needed. You want a nice flowing consistency, so add more breadcrumbs in batches as needed. Keep warm.

Gravy
Put all the vegetables in a large saucepan and sweat in the olive oil. Add the giblets and bones, and cook for a few minutes. Deglaze the pan with the port and Madeira.

Add the water, bay leaves and parsley stalks. Season with salt and pepper. Boil until reduced by half, and strain into a clean saucepan.

Grouse
Pre-heat the oven to 240°C/475°F/gas mark 9.
Season the birds inside and out.

Heat the olive oil in a large frying pan and brown the birds. Remove to a roasting tin and roast in the oven for 10–12 minutes, or cooked to your liking.

Remove the birds from the oven and rest in a warm place for 5 minutes. Strain the pan juices into the gravy and check the flavour; if it needs it, a little beef stock will help the strength.

Serve the birds with the gravy and bread sauce on the side. Accompany with roasted potatoes and parsnips.

SAUTÉ OF SWEETBREADS WITH MORELS

Serves 4

Sauté
1 leek
2 sticks celery
1 large carrot
1 onion
50 g / 2 oz / ¼ cup butter
1 bay leaf
1 tbsp thyme
750 g / 1½ lb sweetbreads, soaked overnight
1.75 litres / 3 pints / 7½ cups light chicken stock
  (see page 136)
4 tbsp olive oil for frying
4 tbsp seasoned flour

Sauce
75 g / 3 oz / ½ cup shallots, chopped
1 garlic clove, crushed
4 tbsp Madeira
300 ml / 10 fl oz / 1¼ cups veal stock (see page 136)
100 g / 4 oz / ½ cup fresh morels, or 40 g / 1½ oz / ¼ cup
  dried re-constituted morels
300 ml / 10 fl oz / 1¼ cups double (heavy) cream
1–2 tbsp parsley, chopped

Sauté
Dice the leek, celery, carrot and onion, place in a large saucepan and sweat in the butter. When cooked, add the bay leaf and thyme, and place the sweetbreads on top. Pour over the chicken stock to cover, bring to the boil, reduce the heat and gently simmer for 3–5 minutes.

Leave to cool in the stock. When cold put the sweetbreads only in a container, cover with clingfilm and place a plate on top. Put weights – not too heavy – on the plate. Place in the refrigerator to set overnight.

The aim is to squeeze the liquid out. Next day, carefully remove the membrane and trim. Cut, at an angle, into 2.5 cm / 1 in slices, allowing three pieces per person.

Heat the olive oil in a frying pan, toss the sweetbreads in the seasoned flour and when the oil is hot, cook until golden brown and cooked through. Drain on absorbent paper and keep warm.

Sauce
Add the shallots and garlic to the oil in the pan, cook for a few seconds, then deglaze with the Madeira, stirring all the time. Add the stock and reduce by half.

Strain into a clean pan, then add the morels and cream. Cook until thick. Check the seasoning. Remove the morels from the sauce.

Lay the sweetbreads down the centre of each plate and place the drained morels on top. Add one tablespoon of parsley to the sauce. Check the flavour then spoon over the sweetbreads and morels. Serve with mashed potatoes.

MAIN COURSES

VEAL KIDNEYS WITH SHALLOTS, PANCETTA AND THYME

Serves 4

2 veal kidneys weighing approx. 750 g / 1¹/₂ lb in total
4–6 tbsp goose or duck fat
100 g / 4 oz / ³/₄ cup shallots, chopped
1 clove garlic, chopped
150 ml / 5 fl oz / ²/₃ cup red wine
175 g / 6 oz pancetta, cut into strips
300 ml / 10 fl oz / 1¹/₄ cups veal stock (see page 136)
350 g / 12 oz tomatoes, skinned, seeded and chopped
2 tbsp fresh thyme leaves
Salt and freshly ground black pepper

Skin the kidneys, remove the core and slice each into four pieces. Melt the fat in a heavy pan and sear the kidneys quickly, keeping them pink. Remove and keep warm.

Add the shallots and garlic to the pan and stir for a few seconds. Add the red wine and stir until well reduced.

Add the pancetta and cook for a few seconds, then add the stock. Reduce by a third and season.

Add the tomatoes and one tablespoon of the thyme. Heat through, and check the seasoning.

Arrange the kidneys on each plate, pour over the sauce and sprinkle with the remaining thyme.

BEEF FILLET WITH MARROW AND RED WINE SAUCE

Serves 4

750 g / 1¹/₂ lb marrow bones, split
100 g / 4 oz / ³/₄ cup shallots, finely chopped
2 tbsp parsley, chopped
4 x 175 g / 6 oz fillet steaks
Salt and freshly ground black pepper
2 tbsp clarified butter
300 ml / 10 fl oz / 1¹/₄ cups good-quality red wine
300 ml / 10 fl oz / 1¹/₄ cups veal stock (see page 136)

Scrape the marrow out of the bones, put into a saucepan and dissolve over a low heat. When dissolved, strain carefully into a frying pan, making sure no bone shards go through.

Sauté half the shallots in the marrow over a medium heat. When transparent, remove from the heat, add the chopped parsley, season and cool.

When completely cold and set, shape into a cylinder and wrap tightly in clingfilm. Chill in the refrigerator.

Season the steaks and heat a large frying pan until very hot. Cook the steaks according to preference and keep warm.

Put the clarified butter and the remaining shallots in the frying pan and cook over a high heat, stirring continuously. Deglaze the pan with the red wine, add the veal stock and reduce until thick. Check the seasoning and strain.

Slice the marrow, place a slice on top of each steak and pour the sauce around.

BAKED APPLE WITH SULTANAS AND CALVADOS

Serves 4

4 Bramley apples, cored but not peeled
50 g / 2 oz / ¼ cup butter, at room temperature
50 g / 2 oz / ⅓ cup sultanas
50 g / 2 oz / ⅓ cup raisins
2 tsp mixed spice
Zest of 1 orange, juice of ½ orange
75 g / 3 oz / ⅓ cup soft brown sugar
4 tbsp Calvados
Vanilla ice-cream, to serve

Pre-heat the oven to 175°C/350°F/gas mark 4.

Stand the apples in a well-greased roasting tin.

Put the butter, sultanas, raisins, spice and orange zest in a mixing bowl and combine. Stuff the centre of each apple with this mixture; sprinkle with the orange juice and sugar.

Pour a spoonful of Calvados over each apple and bake for 45 minutes–1 hour, until the apples are soft and the sugar is caramelized.

Pour a little caramel over each, and serve with vanilla ice-cream.

CINNAMON ICE-CREAM

Serves 4

450 ml / 15 fl oz / 2 cups milk
2 cinnamon sticks
150 g / 5 oz / 3/4 cup caster sugar
7 egg yolks
450 ml / 15 fl oz / 2 cups double (heavy) cream
Ground cinnamon

Put the milk and cinnamon sticks into a saucepan and infuse for about 10 minutes over a low heat. Remove from the heat and cool. Strain.

Put the milk, sugar and egg yolks together in a saucepan. Beat together and cook slowly until thick and coating the back of a spoon. Be careful not to curdle the mixture. Strain and chill.

Half whip the cream and add to the other mixture. Check the flavour and add ground cinnamon as necessary.

Churn in an ice-cream machine, following the manufacturer's instructions. Alternatively, place in a freezer until nearly set, remove, beat with a food mixer and refreeze until set. Remove from the freezer 30 minutes before serving.

WALNUT AND VIEUX PRUNE ICE-CREAM

Serves 4

250 ml / 8 fl oz / 1 cup milk
1/2 vanilla pod
4 egg yolks
75 g / 3 oz / 1/3 cup caster sugar
175 g / 6 oz / 3/4 cup prunes
1 teabag
175 g / 6 oz / 1 1/4 cups walnuts, chopped
3 tbsp Armagnac
175 ml / 6 fl oz / 3/4 cup double (heavy) cream, lightly
*   whipped*

Put the milk and vanilla pod into a pan and infuse for about 10 minutes over a low heat.

Beat the egg yolks and sugar until smooth and pale.

Remove the vanilla pod from the pan and pour the milk on to the egg and sugar mixture. Return to the pan and stir continuously on a gentle heat until the mixture coats the back of a wooden spoon. Remove from the heat and leave to cool. Place the prunes and a teabag in a heatproof bowl and cover with boiling water. Soak overnight, or until soft. Remove the stones and chop the prunes.

Combine the chopped prunes, walnuts and Armagnac and add this mixture to the vanilla custard. Then carefully fold in the whipped cream. Churn for 20 minutes in an ice-cream maker according to the manufacturer's instructions. Alternatively, place in a freezer until nearly set. Remove, beat with a food mixer, and re-freeze until set.

Remove from the freezer 20–30 minutes before serving.

St Emilion au Chocolat

Serves 4

450 g / 1 lb good-quality dark chocolate
250 ml / 8 fl oz / 1 cup milk
225 g / 8 oz / 1 cup unsalted butter
175 g / 6 oz / 2/3 cup caster sugar
2 egg yolks
225 g / 8 oz / 2 cups amaretti biscuits, crushed
2 tbsp Amaretto liqueur
1 tbsp icing sugar
Jersey or whipped cream, to serve

Put the chocolate and milk in a saucepan and dissolve over a low heat. Remove from heat when dissolved.

In a bowl, beat the butter and sugar together until pale and creamy. Beat in the egg yolks then add the chocolate and milk. Line a 15 cm/6 in round springform tin with clingfilm. Cover the base of the tin with half of the Amaretti and sprinkle with the amaretto. Then cover with the chocolate mixture and chill in the refrigerator overnight.

Remove from the tin and peel away the clingfilm. Cover the top of the chocolate with the remaining amaretti and dust with icing sugar. Serve with Jersey cream or softly whipped cream.

Steamed Marmalade Sponge

Serves 4

100 g / 4 oz / 1/2 cup unsalted butter
2 tbsp icing sugar, sifted
100 g / 4 oz / 1/2 cup caster sugar
2 eggs
175 g / 6 oz / 1 1/4 cups plain flour, sifted
1 tsp baking powder
3–4 tbsp milk
4 heaped tsp good-quality marmalade
Custard or double (heavy) cream, to serve

Butter four 200 ml/7 fl oz/1 cup pudding basins and dust with icing sugar.

In a bowl, cream the caster sugar and remaining butter together. Beat in the eggs. Sift the flour, and beat it into the egg mixture with the baking powder. Add the milk, to make a dropping consistency.

Put 1 heaped teaspoon of marmalade into each pudding basin, and place the sponge mixture on top. Cover with foil that has a crease along its middle to allow for rising.

Place the basins in the top of a steamer or double boiler over simmering water. Alternatively, put the basins in a heavy-based pan and add boiling water to the pan to come three-quarters of the way up the sides of the basins. Cover and cook for 30–40 minutes, making sure to replenish with boiling water when necessary. Allow to rest a few minutes before turning out. Serve with custard or cream.

CHOCOLATE AND HAZELNUT TART

Serves 4

¹/₂ quantity sweet pastry (see page 142)
50 g / 2 oz / ¹/₂ cup hazelnuts
75 g / 3 oz / ¹/₃ cup caster sugar
1 egg
2 egg yolks
1 tbsp icing sugar
185 g / 6¹/₂ oz dark chocolate
90 g / 3¹/₂ oz / ¹/₂ cup unsalted butter
Chocolate shavings
Vanilla Anglaise, to serve (see page 91)

Pre-heat the oven to 160°C/325°F/gas mark 3.

Roll out the pastry thinly to line a 20 cm/8 in tart tin. Chill for at least 30 minutes in the refrigerator. Line with greaseproof paper and baking beans. Bake blind for 20–25 minutes. Remove paper and beans and allow to cool.

Meanwhile, heat 50 g/2 oz/¹/₄ cup caster sugar and the hazelnuts together in a saucepan at medium heat until the sugar melts and is golden. Taking care as the mixture will be very hot, pour the sugar and hazelnuts on to an oiled oven tray. Allow to cool, then finely crush the praline.

Cover the pastry base with half the praline and put to one side. Turn the oven down to 110°C/225°F/gas mark 4.

In a bowl, beat the egg, egg yolks and icing sugar together until very thick and pale. Gently fold the chocolate and egg mixture together. Pour into the pastry case and bake for 4 minutes.

Remove from the oven, cool, and place in the refrigerator to set.

Sprinkle the tart with the remaining praline mixture and serve dusted with icing sugar, chocolate shavings and Vanilla Anglaise. Best served at room temperature.

PASSION FRUIT TART WITH CRÈME FRAÎCHE

Serves 4

¹/₂ quantity sweet pastry (see page 142)
18 passion fruit, cut in half
4 eggs
75 g / 3 oz / ¹/₃ cup caster sugar
120 ml / 4 fl oz / ¹/₂ cup double (heavy) cream
2 tbsp icing sugar, sifted
Crème fraîche, to serve

Pre-heat the oven to 160°C/325°F/gas mark 3.

Roll out the pastry thinly to line a 20 cm/8 in fluted flan ring. Chill for at least half an hour in the refrigerator. Line with greaseproof paper and baking beans. Bake blind for 20–25 minutes. Remove paper and beans and allow to cool.

Scrape all the seeds and pulp from fourteen of the passion fruit into a saucepan and warm over a gentle heat, then sieve to separate the juice from the seeds (heating helps to separate the seeds). There should be 85 ml/3 fl oz/¹/₃ cup of juice. Whisk three eggs and the caster sugar together by hand or with a food mixer, then add the cream and the passion fruit juice.

Beat the fourth egg and brush it over the bottom of the tart case.

Strain the egg mixture into the tart case and bake for 30–45 minutes, until just set.

When cool, sprinkle with icing sugar and cut with a hot knife. Arrange a slice on each plate and put a generous spoon of crème fraîche on the side. Garnish with the remaining passion fruit. Serve at room temperature.

CANTINA
DEL PONTE

'It's gutsy food. You have to be hungry to eat it'
Louis Loizia

Cantina del Ponte is a Mediterranean-style trattoria abutting Le Pont de la Tour at the downstream end of the Butlers Wharf Building. The site had originally been earmarked for Le Pont de la Tour but on second thoughts Conran moved Le Pont de la Tour, epicentre of the Gastrodrome, further upstream into the heart of the Butlers Wharf Building.

Cantina's genesis lay in an approach to Conran by Louis Loizia, an operatically 'Greek' ex-St Martin's art student born and raised in Shepherd's Bush who speaks with a broad west London accent. After seven years in Australia where he worked with Tony Bilson, Loizia trained under Santiago Gonzalez, chef at the Neal Street Restaurant, then chefed at Zuma restaurant (now Albero y Grana), a fleeting venture in Chelsea Cloisters, where he brushed with the Milanese master Gualtiero Marchesi. Santiago Gonzalez held that Loizia's talents merited their own restaurant and contacted Conran.

There were no immediate plans for a Mediterranean wing at Butlers Wharf, but Conran felt 'in the mood' to open a simple, earthy, trattoria-like restaurant. He was impressed by Loizia's range of dishes recorded in scrapbooks of photographs, drawings and descriptions that chronicle – in 'catalogue' form – Loizia's travels, and thought he could erect a restaurant that served this type of food.

Compared with the protracted battle to get Butlers Wharf up and running, Cantina's six-month gestation was simple. But Conran and Kissin were unstoppable, now in the full flow of realizing their dreams for the Gastrodrome.

At the door, a pizza counter is addressed by wood-topped, galvanized-metal stools. In the main body of the room simple wood tables, designed by Conran and made by Benchmark, have hard-wearing maple tops. Beech and cane chairs are built to an English design in northern Italy. Mexican terracotta tiles line the floor. In fine weather the floor-to-ceiling windows open up to let sunlight wash in. By night, aquamarine and white deckchair-stripe curtains are drawn and fine lights from tiny spotlights dangle from 'fishing rods' that angle out into mid-room, highlighting well-groomed young heads. 'It's not a lingering restaurant,'

says Conran. 'It's meant to have the feel of a simple seaside trattoria. The square tables are saying "eat and go".'

The main feature of Cantina's interior is Timna Woollard's mural of the progression of food from cargo to kitchen which covers the entire length of the rear wall, and which Conran considers the finest piece of decorative art in the Gastrodrome. In warm colours of brown, rusty red, cream and terracotta, it charts the traffic of foodstuffs from river barges via market stalls to kitchens and into the hands of chefs in a 1920s-style 'Mediterranean' interpretation of the history of Butlers Wharf. Conran's brief to Timna Woollard was to 'give it plenty of energy and activity'. 'Terence Conran discovered "cantina" meant cellar, so I had to put a wine cellar at one end.'

A small, white-tiled bar marks the entrance to the Cantina and acts mainly as a service area for customers' drinks orders.

Coincidentally, Timna Woollard trained at art school with Louis Loizia, Cantina's chef. The food at Cantina is a rendition of traditional Italian, Greek and Spanish dishes, with powerful influences from the classics, as well as from Australian (or 'Pacific Rim') cooking. As Loizia explains, 'Saffron risotto is a classic north Italian dish. In Italy they turn the leftovers into a flat pancake served fried – the Italian version of bubble and squeak. In the Pan-fried Saffron Risotto I adapt it and accompany it with wild mushrooms. Plum Tomato Timbale with Pesto was a dish I ate in Milan, served in a ramekin as a starter. I've put it in a dariole mould that you can turn out. Zucchini flowers are normally served fried in Italy. I've stuffed them with mashed potatoes, capers, celery, chopped tomatoes, sun-dried tomatoes and parsley, then steamed them. I ate red mullet fresh from the sea as a child in Cyprus, and thought that grilled red mullet would work well with another classic, Fennel and Orange Salad. When fennel and oranges are in season they're normally served as an appetizer, but they're a good accompaniment to fish and poultry. Sweet and Sour Onions [with Sautéed Calves' Liver] are found in most delicatessens in northern Italy.

They're easy to cook and go well with liver. Red Wine Sausages, Haloumi and Fried Duck Eggs is a Greek-Cypriot dish which includes two items that my mother used to make: red wine sausages and haloumi, which is dried cows' milk cheese made out of milk brought to the boil and set with rennet. Eight pints of milk ·make a twelve-ounce haloumi. Chocolate Panettone Bread and Butter Pudding comes from a recipe for chocolate bread which I adapted. Panna Cotta with mixed Berries is a northern Italian recipe: I've eaten this dish all over Italy and most of them are like glue. Mine is the best.

'If you discipline yourself, 80 per cent of the recipes are straightforward. You just have to get the finest ingredients and not abuse them. It's gutsy food. You have to be hungry.'

A model of Tower Bridge stranded on a sandbank dominates the upstream end of the restaurant. The sandbank stretches the whole depth of the restaurant, and is contained by an angled glass shelf.

CANTINA
DEL PONTE

STARTERS

Pan-fried Saffron Risotto with Mixed Mushrooms
Stuffed Courgette Flowers
Plum Tomato Timbale with Pesto
Rigatoni with Gorgonzola, Courgettes and Baby Artichokes
Porcini Mushroom Ravioli
Deep-fried Calamari with Taramasalata and Cucumbers

MAIN COURSES

Red Onion, Fontina and Black Olive Pizza
Red Mullet with Fennel and Orange Salad
Swordfish with a Salad of Green Beans, Tomatoes, Red Onions
and Black Olives
Flattened Poussin with Courgette and Red Pepper Casserole
Roast Duck with Peas, Garlic and Rosemary Potatoes
Veal Escalope with Chicory, Mozzarella, Spinach and Parmesan
Green Juniper and Red Wine Sausages with Haloumi
and Fried Duck Eggs
Sautéed Calves' Liver with Sweet and Sour Onions

DESSERTS

Blood Orange Jelly with Citrus Salad
Zabaglione Ice-cream
Chocolate Panettone Bread anad Butter Pudding
Fig and Cinnamon Tart
Chocolate and Coffee Cone with Vanilla Anglaise
Panna Cotta with Mixed Berries

CANTINA
DEL PONTE

PAN-FRIED SAFFRON RISOTTO WITH MIXED MUSHROOMS ✪

Serves 4

Risotto

450 ml / 15 fl oz / 2 cups dry white wine
1 tsp / 2 sachets saffron
50 g / 2 oz / 1/3 cup shallots, diced
50 g / 2 oz / 1/4 cup clarified butter
350 g / 12 oz / 1 3/4 cups carnaroli rice
900 ml / 1 1/2 pints / 3 1/2 cups good chicken or vegetable stock
    (see page 136)
100 g / 4 oz / 1 cup Parmesan cheese, grated
75 g / 3 oz / 1/3 cup butter, softened
4 eggs, lightly beaten

Mixed Mushrooms

1 kg / 2 lb mixed mushrooms, such as shitake, porcini, oyster,
    flat, button
6 tbsp clarified butter mixed with
3 tbsp olive oil
2 garlic cloves, chopped
65 ml / 2 1/2 fl oz / 1/4 cup white wine
2 tbsp curly parsley, chopped
50 g / 2 oz / 1/4 cup butter, diced, at room temperature
1/2 tsp sea salt
Freshly ground black pepper

Risotto

Pour the white wine into a measuring jug and infuse the saffron.

Put the shallots in a large saucepan and sauté in the clarified butter until transparent. Add the rice and cook gently until slightly translucent. Add three-quarters of the white wine infusion, saving a generous splash for later. Simmer until the wine reduces by half, stirring all the time.

Bring the wine stock to the boil. Then slowly add the chicken or vegetable stock to the mixture, a ladleful at a time, while stirring constantly.

When the rice is just about cooked (al dente), add the remaining wine and the Parmesan. Still stirring, gradually work in the softened butter.

Let the rice continue to cook until soft but not losing its shape. Allow the mixture to cool to room temperature, then mix in the eggs, and refrigerate.

Mixed Mushrooms

Tear the mushrooms by hand into 2.5 cm / 1 in pieces. Place them in a large saucepan with the butter and oil and sauté them over a medium high heat. Stir until they begin to soften and give up their liquor. Reduce the heat to low and let them cook until almost dry.

Add the garlic, cook for a further 2 minutes, then pour in the wine. Bring to the boil to evaporate the alcohol and then remove from the heat and keep in a warm place until needed.

To Finish

The chilled rice mixture can be formed into either four small cakes, or one large one, depending on preference, and this is easiest done using hands rinsed in cold water. Fry the cakes over a medium to low heat until a golden crust forms (approx 7 minutes) – avoiding the temptation to try to turn them over before the mixture has set – then flip them over and fry on the other side.

When you are ready to serve, reheat the mushrooms until the mixture starts to bubble gently, then add the chopped parsley and swirl in the diced butter to thicken the mixture. Season to taste with salt and plenty of fresh black pepper, and spoon the mushroom sauce over the risotto cakes.

The risotto is best made the day before. You can also prepare the mushrooms the day before. This makes the dish very quick to assemble.

STARTERS

STUFFED COURGETTE FLOWERS

Serves 4

450 g / 1 lb potatoes, peeled and diced
Salt and freshly ground black pepper
8 courgettes (zucchini), with flower attached
2 tbsp baby capers, rinsed and drained
2 tbsp celery, finely diced
2 tbsp tomatoes, finely diced
1 tbsp sun-dried tomatoes, cut into strips
1 tbsp flat-leaf parsley, coarsely chopped
1 tbsp salted anchovy, chopped

Put the potatoes in a saucepan, cover with cold water and add salt. Bring to the boil and simmer for 12–15 minutes or until very soft. Drain well and pass through a sieve into a mixing bowl. Keep on one side.

Gently wash the courgette flowers in salted water to remove any little hairs and insects. Pat dry. The flowers are delicate and need to be kept whole.

When the potato is cold, mix in all the other ingredients and season well. Be careful not to over-salt.

Carefully part the petals of each flower and fill with the potato mixture, wrapping the petals around the stuffing so it is completely covered.

Wrap each courgette in buttered foil or paper. Steam in a steamer over boiling water for 10–15 minutes.

Serve at room temperature or slightly hotter, as part of a selection of antipasti, or on their own on a bed of dressed salad leaves.

PLUM TOMATO TIMBALE WITH PESTO Ⓥ

Serves 4

1.5 kg / 3 lb plum tomatoes, cut into 6
1 tsp sugar
3–5 drops Tabasco sauce
8–10 basil leaves
1 tsp tomato paste or tomato juice
65 ml / 2 1/2 fl oz / 1/4 cup double (heavy) cream
2 1/2 tsp gelatine
4 tbsp pesto (see page 139)
30–40 black olives

Put the tomatoes into a large pan with the sugar and Tabasco and cook until mushy. Add the basil and check the seasoning. Cool slightly. Liquidize the tomatoes in a blender or food processor, then sieve.

Measure the purée: you should have 450–600 ml / 3/4–1 pint / 2–2 1/2 cups. If there is less, add a little tomato paste dissolved in a few spoons of water, or tomato juice.

Warm the cream in a heavy pan. Bring to the boil briefly then remove from the heat and sprinkle on the gelatine. Allow to dissolve, then stir into the tomato mixture. Check the seasoning. Pour into four 200 ml / 7 fl oz / 1 cup moulds, and chill overnight.

Unmould on to individual plates, pour the pesto sauce around and decorate with black olives.

RIGATONI WITH GORGONZOLA, COURGETTES AND BABY ARTICHOKES Ⓥ

Serves 4

225 g / 8 oz / 1 cup marinaded baby artichokes (caroiolini)
Olive oil
225 g / 8 oz / courgettes (zucchini), cut into slices
1 garlic clove, crushed
450 g / 1 lb fresh rigatoni
225 g / 8 oz / 1 cup mascarpone cheese
225 g / 8 oz / 1 cup gorgonzola cheese, cut into 1 cm /
   ¹/₂ in cubes
Salt and freshly ground black pepper
25 g / 1 oz / ¹/₄ cup Parmesan cheese, grated

Drain the artichokes and cut into halves or quarters. The artichokes may be deep-fried, baked or pan-fried depending on your preference. The desired result is that they are golden brown and crisp. Drain and reserve.

Put the oil from the artichoke marinade into a frying pan. If it does not coat the bottom of the pan, add some olive oil. When hot, add the courgettes and garlic, and cook until lightly coloured. Remove from the heat.

Put a large pan of salted water on to boil, then add the rigatoni and cook for about 2 minutes or until *al dente*, and drain.

Put the courgettes back on a high heat, add the mascarpone and gorgonzola and stir; do not boil. In a large bowl, toss the vegetable mixture and the rigatoni together, season, and sprinkle with Parmesan. Place the crisp artichokes on top.

PORCINI MUSHROOM RAVIOLI Ⓥ

Serves 6 as starter, 4 as a main course

450 g / 1 lb / 3 cups plain flour
Salt and freshly ground black pepper
7–8 large eggs, preferably free-range
1 kg / 2 lb porcini mushrooms, or 750 g / 1¹/₂ lb button
   mushrooms and 100 g / 4 oz / 1 cup dried porcini,
   reconstituted
2 tbsp olive oil
2 garlic cloves, chopped
2–3 tbsp parsley, chopped
150 g / 5 oz / 1¹/₄ cups Parmesan cheese, grated
50 g / 2 oz / ¹/₄ cup butter, melted

Sift the flour into a mixing bowl or food processor and add a large pinch of salt. Slowly add five or six eggs until the mixture forms a soft dough. Cover in clingfilm and let it rest in a cool place for at least 1 hour.

Slice the mushrooms into a large saucepan and fry in olive oil with the garlic until any liquid evaporates, then add parsley to taste and remove from the heat. Season.

In a blender or food processor liquidize half the mushrooms and mix in a whole egg, one egg yolk and half of the Parmesan cheese (beat the remaining egg white). The mixture should be cohesive and fairly dry; if necessary, add more Parmesan.

Roll out the dough, preferably using a pasta machine, constantly folding it over on itself until it becomes smooth and slightly silky to the touch.

Divide the dough in two and roll out into thin sheets of the same size. Lay out one sheet on a floured surface and brush with the beaten egg white. Place teaspoons of the mixture at regular intervals on the dough. Lay the second sheet over the top and gently press down around each filling. Cut out the ravioli using a fluted pastry cutter or a pastry wheel.

The ravioli should be cooked in a generous amount of boiling water. When they float to the top they are cooked.

Place some of the cooked, sliced mushrooms on each portion, dust with freshly grated Parmesan, and dribble melted butter over. Serve immediately on warm plates.

DEEP-FRIED CALAMARI WITH TARAMASALATA AND CUCUMBERS

Serves 4

Taramasalata
450 g / 1 lb potatoes, peeled and diced
Salt and freshly ground black pepper
100 g / 4 oz / 3/4 cup smoked cods' roe, skinned
2 lemons, juiced
600 ml / 1 pint / 2 1/2 cups light vegetable oil or light olive oil

Calamari
1 x 360 g / 12 oz packet tempura batter mix
450 g / 1 lb cleaned calamari tubes
1.5 litres / 2 1/2 pints / 6 1/4 cups vegetable oil or light olive oil
4 baby cucumbers, thinly sliced lengthways
Salt and freshly ground black pepper
4 tbsp extra-virgin olive oil
1 lemon, cut into quarters

Taramasalata
Put the potatoes in a saucepan, cover with cold water and add salt. Bring to the boil and simmer for 12–15 minutes or until very soft. Drain well and pass through a sieve.

Mash the skinned cods' roe with a fork in a large bowl. Add the juice of one lemon, the potato purée and plenty of black pepper. Mix together, and slowly add the light vegetable oil, stirring continuously. If the mixture starts to develop a film of oil or slip down the sides of the bowl, stop adding oil, otherwise it will split. The above procedure can be done in a food mixer with the metal whisk attachment, but it must be done slowly, also you may not need all the oil. Add more lemon juice and check seasoning. Refrigerate.

Calamari
Make up the batter according to the instructions on the packet (available from good Oriental food stores).

Slice the calamari into rings by cutting across the tubes. Heat the oil in a large saucepan to 160–180°C/ 320–350°F.

Cook the calamari by dipping the rings in the tempura batter and carefully placing in the hot oil, trailing drips of batter across the frying pieces to create a spiked effect. When golden, remove from the oil and drain.

On four individual plates place a large spoonful of taramasalata and slices of cucumber. Arrange the calamari around the taramasalata and cucumber. Season, dribble with good olive oil and garnish with lemon.

RED ONION, FONTINA AND BLACK OLIVE PIZZA ⓥ

Serves 4

Pizza Dough
65 ml / 2¹/₂ fl oz / ¹/₄ cup water
15 g / ¹/₂ oz fresh yeast
350 g / 12 oz / 2¹/₂ cups plain flour
65 ml / 2¹/₂ fl oz / ¹/₄ cup milk
3 tbsp olive oil
¹/₂ tsp salt

Topping
750 g / 1¹/₂ lb plum tomatoes
Olive oil
Salt and freshly ground black pepper
275 g / 10 oz / 2¹/₄ cups fontina cheese
1 red onion, thinly sliced
15–20 black olives, pitted

Pre-heat the oven to 240°C/475°F/gas mark 9.

Warm the water to blood temperature, pour into a mixing bowl and dissolve the yeast in it. Mix with the flour. Add the milk, olive oil and salt, and knead for at least 15 minutes. Place the dough in a clean bowl, cover with a cloth and leave for 1–2 hours or until it has doubled in size.

Dice the tomatoes coarsely and sweat in olive oil in a large pan. When cooked, liquidize in a blender or food processor and sieve. Season, and keep on one side.

Knead the dough again, then divide into four pieces and press out with fingertips to about 18 cm/7 in diameter. Place on oiled oven trays. Spread the tomato purée over the dough. Slice the fontina and arrange on top of the tomato. Sprinkle with the sliced onion and the black olives, and season.

Bake in a pre-heated oven for 10–15 minutes, or until cooked through. Serve dribbled with olive oil.

RED MULLET WITH FENNEL AND ORANGE SALAD

Serves 4

¹/₂ tbsp lemon thyme
2 lemons, halved and juiced
200 ml / 7 fl oz / 1 cup olive oil
¹/₂ tsp sea salt
1 tsp freshly ground black pepper
2 x 450 g / 1 lb bulbs fennel, very thinly sliced
50 g / 2 oz / ¹/₃ cup plain flour, seasoned
¹/₄ tsp cayenne pepper
4–6 tbsp clarified butter
2 x 750 g / 1¹/₂ lb red mullet, scaled and filleted
6 oranges, peeled and segmented

In a non-metallic container, mix the thyme, lemon juice, olive oil, sea salt and half a teaspoon of pepper and add the fennel. Marinate overnight, or for up to 5 days.

Mix the flour, cayenne pepper and remaining black pepper together.

Heat the butter in a frying pan, toss the fish in the seasoned flour and cook in the butter for about 4 minutes on each side, depending on the thickness. Keep warm.

Drain the fennel, reserve the liquid, and mix with the orange segments. Put a pile on each plate and top with the fish. Dribble with the marinade dressing.

Opposite: Red Mullet with Fennel and Orange Salad

MAIN COURSES

SWORDFISH WITH A SALAD OF GREEN BEANS, TOMATOES, RED ONIONS AND BLACK OLIVES

Serves 4

225 g / 8 oz green beans, topped but not tailed
100 g / 4 oz tomatoes, skinned and seeded
75 g / 3 oz / 1/2 cup black olives
100 g / 4 oz / 3/4 cup red onions, finely sliced
65 ml / 2 1/2 fl oz / 1/4 cup balsamic vinegar
4 x 175 g / 6 oz swordfish steaks, cut from the loin
150 ml / 5 fl oz / 2/3 cup olive oil
Salt and freshly ground black pepper

Bring a pan of salted water to the boil. Blanch the beans until tender, but still slightly crunchy.

Cut the tomatoes into strips and mix with the beans, olives and red onions in a bowl. Dress with balsamic vinegar and olive oil, reserving a little of both for later.

Brush the swordfish with olive oil and grill (broil) or fry until pink: about 4 minutes on each side, depending on thickness.

Place the salad on the plates and arrange the swordfish steaks on top. Dress with a little balsamic vinegar and olive oil, and season.

FLATTENED POUSSIN WITH COURGETTE AND RED PEPPER CASSEROLE

Serves 4

4 poussin

Marinade
75 g / 3 oz / 1/3 cup Dijon mustard
4 cloves garlic, chopped
4 sprigs rosemary, chopped
200 ml / 7 fl oz / 1 cup white wine
300 ml / 10 fl oz / 1 1/4 cups vegetable oil
Salt and freshly ground black pepper

Casserole
4 tbsp olive oil
75 g / 3 oz / 1/2 cup shallots, chopped
550 g / 1 1/4 lb courgettes (zucchini), thinly sliced
1 clove garlic, chopped
100 g / 4 oz sun-dried tomatoes, chopped
5 tomatoes, skinned, seeded and chopped
150 ml / 5 fl oz / 2/3 cup white wine
2 red peppers
Salt and freshly ground black pepper

Marinade
In a bowl, mix together the mustard, garlic and rosemary, stir in the white wine, then slowly add the vegetable oil in a thin stream stirring all the time, as if making mayonnaise. Season.

Poussin and Casserole
Flatten the poussin: remove the spine and cut off the wing-tips. Place skin side up, then press the breastplate down flat until it cracks. Place the flattened poussin in the marinade and leave for at least 3 days, or up to a week.

Heat the olive oil in a large saucepan and fry the shallots for a few minutes, then add the courgettes and garlic. Stir over a medium heat for a few minutes, then add the sun-dried tomatoes, tomatoes and white wine. Cook, stirring all the time until the liquid has reduced by half. Check the seasoning and keep warm.

Grill (broil) the birds for 30–45 minutes, or until the juices run clear when the thigh is pricked.

At the same time, grill (broil) or roast the peppers until the skin is completely black. Remove them from the heat, place in a bowl and cover with clingfilm. Allow them to cool a little, then remove the skins and seeds and cut into thin strips.

Place a quarter of the casserole on each plate, place a bird on top and decorate with strips of red pepper.

Tips
The birds can be marinaded for up to a week ahead.

Poussin is best partly cooked in a hot oven to set the muscles, then finished under a hot grill (broiler).

ROAST DUCK WITH PEAS, GARLIC AND ROSEMARY POTATOES

Serves 4

2 x 1.75 kg / 4 lb ducks
Salt and freshly ground black pepper
1 onion, cut into 2.5 cm / 1 in pieces
1 stick celery, cut into 2.5 cm / 1 in pieces
1 small carrot, cut into 2.5 cm / 1 in pieces
4 tbsp Madeira
600 ml / 1 pint / 2¹/₂ cups good chicken stock (see page 136)
4 tsp fresh thyme or 2 tsp dried thyme
1 kg / 2 lb potatoes, peeled, diced and part-boiled
8 sprigs fresh or 2 tbsp dried rosemary
2 garlic cloves, peeled and sliced
450 g / 1 lb fine peas, blanched

Pre-heat the oven to 240°C/475°F/gas mark 9.

Lightly score the duck skin, and rub salt inside and out. Place both birds in the same roasting tin, breast side up. Place in the oven and cook for 20 minutes, then turn over, breast side down (they will tilt to one side). Cook on one side for 20 minutes, then tilt them on the other side and cook for a further 20 minutes. For the last 20 minutes lay the ducks on their backs to crisp the breast skin. Remove from the oven and rest. Strain and reserve the duck fat. Turn the oven down to 200°C/400°F/gas mark 6.

Place two tablespoons of duck fat in a saucepan, then add the onion, celery and carrot. Brown the vegetables. Deglaze the pan with two tablespoons of Madeira, add the chicken stock and bring to the boil.

When the birds are cool enough to handle, cut in half lengthways and remove the spine and rib cage. Add the bones and thyme to the stock and reduce until thick. Place the four duck halves back in the roasting tin.

MAIN COURSES

Pour four tablespoons of duck fat in a roasting tin and place in the oven. When smoking, add the part-boiled potatoes. Cook for 20 minutes then turn them over. The potatoes will take about 30–45 minutes to cook. Fifteen minutes before they are ready, put the duck halves in the lower part of the oven to warm through, and add the rosemary and garlic to the potatoes. Strain the sauce, add the rest of the Madeira and check the seasoning.

Put the peas in a saucepan with a little salted water and cook for about 5 minutes or until cooked through but not soft. Drain.

Mix the peas with the sauce and put on each plate. Sit the duck on top with the potatoes on the side.

VEAL ESCALOPE WITH CHICORY, MOZZARELLA, SPINACH AND PARMESAN

Serves 4

4 x 175 g / 6 oz veal escalopes
25 g / 1 oz / 1/4 cup seasoned flour
2 eggs, beaten
175 g / 6 oz / 3 cups dry breadcrumbs
4 tbsp clarified butter
2 tbsp olive oil
4 heads chicory, quartered with core removed
350 g / 12 oz mozzarella cheese, cut into 12 slices
Salt and freshly ground black pepper
225 g / 8 oz puisse épinard (baby spinach)
75 g / 3 oz piece of Parmesan cheese
2 lemons, cut into quarters

Coat the veal in the seasoned flour, dip into the egg, cover completely with the breadcrumbs and chill for at least 30 minutes.

Heat two tablespoons of the butter in a large frying pan. When hot, brown two slices of veal on both sides. Keep warm, wipe out the pan with kitchen paper and cook the other two slices in the same way and keep warm. Wipe the pan clean with a paper towel.

Heat the olive oil in the frying pan. When nearly smoking, add the chicory and toss, then throw in the mozzarella and toss again. Finally, add the spinach, season and toss. You only want the leaves to wilt, not to cook too much.

Place a quarter of this mixture on each plate, and top with a piece of veal. Garnish with shavings of Parmesan, and place pieces of lemon on the side.

MAIN COURSES

GREEK JUNIPER AND RED WINE SAUSAGES WITH HALOUMI AND FRIED DUCK EGGS

Serves 4

1.25 kg / 2¹/₂ lb belly of pork, coarsely minced
¹/₂ tsp Greek juniper berries
¹/₂ tsp dried oregano
¹/₂ tsp ground cinnamon
¹/₂ tsp salt
750 ml / 1¹/₄ pints / 3 cups red wine
25 g / 1 oz sausage skins, or 8 pieces of caul fat
350 g / 12 oz haloumi cheese, cut into 8 slices
4 duck eggs
Vegetable oil for frying
Warm bread, to serve

Mix the minced pork with the juniper berries, oregano, cinnamon and salt. Stir in the red wine, cover and leave in the refrigerator overnight.

Next day, fill the skins with the pork mixture, using a piping bag. Shape into eight lengths and tie with string.

Hang the sausages in a cool, airy place to dry for a few days, or wrap in brown paper and keep in the refrigerator. Cook when dry.

Fry the sausages in a little oil for 10 minutes, or until cooked. Remove and keep warm. Fry the haloumi cheese in the same pan until coloured. Remove and keep warm. Fry the eggs, keeping the yolks runny. Serve the sausage, haloumi and eggs together with warm bread.

SAUTÉED CALVES' LIVER WITH SWEET AND SOUR ONIONS

Serves 4

450 g / 1 lb button onions, peeled
100 g / 4 oz / ¹/₂ cup softened butter
50 g / 2 oz / ¹/₄ cup sugar, white
4 tbsp white wine vinegar
8 x 75 g / 3 oz slices veal liver, seasoned
Salt and freshly ground black pepper
100 g / 4 oz / ¹/₂ cup clarified butter

Pre-heat the oven to 180°C/350°F/gas mark 4.

Place the onions, softened butter, white sugar and vinegar in a roasting pan. Season with salt and pepper. Cover with foil and place in the oven for 30–45 minutes, depending on the size of the onions. When nearly tender, pour everything into a frying pan, and on a high heat, toss the onions until nicely browned and the juices have reduced to a glaze. Keep warm.

Fry the calves' liver in the clarified butter until browned on both sides. The time needed depends on how well you like liver to be cooked (approximately 2 minutes on each side for bloody, up to 5 minutes on each side for well done). Serve garnished with the sweet and sour onions.

BLOOD ORANGE JELLY WITH CITRUS SALAD

Serves 4

600 ml / 1 pint / 2¹/₂ cups blood orange juice
4 tsp gelatine
50–100 g / 2–4 oz / ¹/₄–¹/₂ cup sugar
3 tbsp Cointreau
1 lemon, juiced
350–450 g / 12–16 oz citrus fruit (orange, grapefruit,
*   lime), peeled and segmented*

Warm half of the orange juice then sprinkle on the gelatine. When dissolved, stir in the sugar, Cointreau, lemon juice and remaining orange juice. Pour into four 200 ml / 7 fl oz / 1 cup dariole moulds and chill overnight.

   Unmould on to plates and surround with the citrus fruits.

ZABAGLIONE ICE-CREAM

Serves 4

450 ml / 15 fl oz / 2 cups double (heavy) cream
450 ml / 15 fl oz / 2 cups milk
12 egg yolks
75–100 g / 3–4 oz / ¹/₃– ¹/₂ cup caster sugar
4 tbsp Marsala, or to taste
Almond biscuits, to serve

Put the cream, milk, egg yolks and sugar in a saucepan and cook on a medium heat, stirring all the time, until you have a thick custard that coats the back of a spoon. Cool.

   Add the Marsala and churn in an ice-cream machine, following the manufacturer's instructions.

   Serve with almond biscuits.

CHOCOLATE PANETTONE BREAD AND BUTTER PUDDING

Serves 4–6

225 g / 8 oz panettone or brioche (see page 141)
225 g / 8 oz plain chocolate
450 ml / 15 fl oz / 2 cups double (heavy) cream
4 egg yolks
50 g / 2 oz / ¹/₄ cup caster sugar
50 g / 2 oz / ¹/₄ cup brown sugar
Clotted or whipped (heavy) cream, to serve

Pre-heat the oven to 190°C/375°F/gas mark 5. Cut the panettone into 1 cm/¹/₂ in slices.

   Melt the chocolate and cream together in a basin over simmering water. In a separate bowl, whisk the egg yolks and caster sugar together until pale.

   Mix the cream and chocolate into the yolk mixture and return to the basin over the pan of simmering water. Lower the heat, and stir continuously until the mixture is thick and coats the back of a wooden spoon.

   Pour a little of this mixture into the bottom of a 1 litre/2 pint/4 cup ovenproof dish and layer with the panettone. Continue layers, making sure that the top layer of panettone is coated with the custard so that it remains moist. Leave to rest for 1 hour or longer – even overnight.

   Place the dish in a roasting tin and pour boiling water into the tin until it comes halfway up the dish's sides.

   Cook in the oven for approximately 45 minutes, or until set.

   Remove from the oven and cover the pudding with an even layer of brown sugar. Place under a hot grill (broiler) to caramelize the sugar. Leave for a few minutes to allow the sugar to set.

   Serve with clotted or softly whipped cream.

FIG AND CINNAMON TART

Serves 4

Filling
300 ml / 10 fl oz / 1¼ cups double (heavy) cream
40 g / 1½ oz / ¼ cup caster sugar
½ cinnamon stick
1 tsp cinnamon
2 tsp gelatine
3 tbsp milk
6 ripe figs, sliced
4 tbsp runny honey

Sweet Pastry
150 g / 5 oz / 1 cup plain flour, sieved
100 g / 2 oz / ¼ cup unsalted butter
65 g / 2½ oz / ⅓ cup caster sugar
1 egg yolk

Filling
Put the cream, sugar, cinnamon stick and ground cinnamon into a saucepan. Bring briefly to the boil, then remove from the heat. Dissolve the gelatine in the milk, and add to the cinnamon cream. Sieve into a bowl and chill overnight.

Once set, whip the mixture until it thickens and forms peaks, like whipped cream.

Sweet Pastry
Work the flour, butter, sugar and egg yolk together in a mixing bowl until you have a dough. Place in the refrigerator to chill.

Pre-heat the oven to 200°C/400°F/gas mark 6.

Roll out the pastry and cut it to fit four 11.5cm/4½ in flan tins. Bake blind until nicely golden (about 15–20 minutes). Allow to cool.

When cold, assemble the tarts by putting cinnamon cream in the bottom of the tart case and arranging the sliced figs on top. Dribble with honey.

CHOCOLATE AND COFFEE CONE WITH VANILLA ANGLAISE

Makes 8 cones

Chocolate and Coffee Pastry Cream
150 ml / 5 fl oz / ½ cup double (heavy) cream
150 ml / 5 fl oz / ½ cup milk
100 g / 4 oz dark chocolate
3 tbsp very strong coffee (espresso)
4 egg yolks
100 g / 4 oz / ½ cup caster sugar
50 g / 2 oz / ⅓ cup plain flour, sieved
2 tbsp Tia Maria
200 g / 7 oz / 1 cup mascarpone cheese

Cones
50 g / 2 oz / ¼ cup golden syrup
50 g / 2 oz / ¼ cup butter
50 g / 2 oz / ¼ cup caster sugar
Juice from ¼ lemon
40 g / 1½ oz / ¼ cup plain flour, sieved
2 tbsp cocoa, sieved

Vanilla Anglaise
300 ml / 10 fl oz / 1¼ cups double (heavy) cream
½ vanilla pod, split lengthways
4 egg yolks
40 g / 1½ oz / ¼ cup caster sugar
24 coffee beans, roasted

Chocolate and Coffee Pastry Cream
Put the cream, milk, chocolate and coffee in a saucepan and bring to the boil.

In a bowl, whisk the egg yolks and sugar together. Add the flour and whisk to a smooth paste. Pour the cream mixture into the egg mixture, stir, and return to the pan. Beat the cream on a low heat until you have a thick custard that will coat the back of a spoon.

Remove from the heat and add the Tia Maria. Put clingfilm on the surface of the sauce (to stop a skin forming). Place in the refrigerator to set.

When set, fold in the mascarpone and chill in the refrigerator.

Cones

Pre-heat the oven to 200°C/400°F/gas mark 6.

In a saucepan melt together the syrup, butter, sugar and lemon juice. Remove from the heat and stir in the flour and cocoa. Allow to cool.

Place two teaspoons of the mixture on an oven tray lined with silicone paper. Put in the middle of the oven and cook for 5–10 minutes. The mixture will spread to about 15 cm/6 in diameter. Cool slightly, shape into a cone and cool.

Do this with all the mixture. Be careful as the cones are quite delicate.

Vanilla Anglaise

Put the cream into a saucepan, add the vanilla pod and briefly bring to the boil. Remove from the heat.

In a bowl, whisk together the egg yolks and sugar. Whisk the cream into the yolk mixture, return it to the pan and cook until it coats the back of a spoon. Strain, and chill in the refrigerator.

To assemble, put a pool of Anglaise on each plate, fill the cones with the pastry cream, and place on top. Garnish with the coffee beans.

PANNA COTTA WITH MIXED BERRIES

Serves 4

Panna Cotta
600 ml / 1 pint / 2½ cups double (heavy) cream
50 g / 2 oz / ¼ cup sugar
½ vanilla pod, split lengthways
2 tsp gelatine
3 tbsp milk

Berries
350 g / 12 oz / 3½ cups raspberries, fresh or frozen
50–75 g / 2–4 oz / ¼–½ cup icing sugar, or to taste
Raspberry liqueur, to taste (optional)
450 g / 1 lb / 4½ cups mixed fresh berries
2–3 tbsp icing sugar, to dust

Panna Cotta

Put the cream in a heavy saucepan and bring to the boil with the split vanilla pod and sugar. Once the mixture has come to the boil, remove from the heat. Dissolve the gelatine in the milk, and add it to the cream.

Strain, then pour into four 200 ml/7 fl oz/1 cup dariole moulds. When cold, refrigerate (overnight) until set.

Berries

Process the raspberries in a blender or food processor with the icing sugar and optional liqueur, until the fruit softens to a purée. Sieve, and stir in the mixed berries.

To serve the panna cotta, run a knife around the edge of the moulds and dip them into hot water for 10 seconds. Turn out on to individual plates with the berries on the side. Dust with the remaining icing sugar.

Panna Cotta with Mixed Berries

THE BUTLERS WHARF

Chop House

'Taking the best of British food and getting rid of
the stodgy overcooked vegetables'

Rod Eggleston

The most recent tier to the Gastrodrome is the Butlers Wharf Chop-house, situated upstream of Le Pont de la Tour on the ground floor of the Butlers Wharf Building. Chop-house is a generic English name like 'pub'. There were once thousands of chop-houses in London in the seventeenth and eighteenth centuries and it seemed appropriate to bring one back again under the shadow of Tower Bridge. The all-wood interior, a glowing tribute to British dendrophilia, is like walking into a faintly aromatic cigar box.

In 1992, having just completed his design for Quaglino's, Conran retreated to Barton Court to sketch plans for a restaurant devoted to 'really good British food'. The design was complete in a little over five days.

'I wanted the Chop-house to attract the City but not in a repro way and without having to resort to dark mahogany, etched glass, dark-red plush, brass and Bateman cartoons,' says Conran. 'I wanted to progress. I was thinking about "modern Englishness" and about St Ives and Truro in the pre- and post-war years, and the influence of Ben Nicholson, Barbara Hepworth, Bernard Leach and Eric Ravillious; and about the modern English aesthetic notions of Henry Moore.

You enter the Chop-house via the Chop Shop where the smell of sizzling beef, home-made sausages, chutneys, pickles and preserves sets the tastebuds alight. Moving into the Chop-house bar, you confront a world seemingly devoted entirely to wood.

There's a hail-fellow-well-met feel to the heavy high-backed oaken settles with soft red leather seats and sprung backs of slatted ash made by Benchmark. You can imagine a latterday Falstaff holding forth to a company of rapt companions seated on chairs based on a classic eighteenth-century design reworked in a mixture of ash and elm. 'The chair is a derivation of a tradi-tional bodger's Windsor chair,' says Conran. 'They used to make chairs in the beech woods of Wycombe in the eighteenth century. I took an existing Windsor chair and used that as the base for the design. I found a bodger in Farringdon who made it for us.'

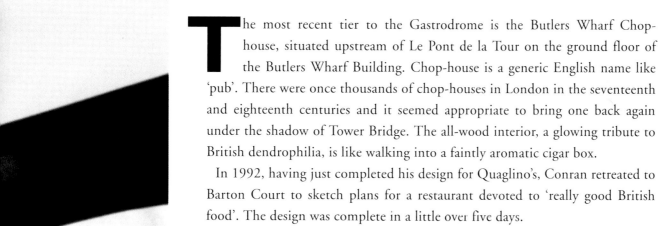

Floors, chairs, tables and wall-fittings are all hewn from radiant timber with scarcely a dab of paint in sight.

Opposite: The imposing presence of Tower Bridge is an inescapable feature of the landscape of the Gastrodrome.

Already the pre-distressed zinc tabletops in the bar are wearing themselves in nicely. With each spilt drop of beer or wine, the acid contained in the alcohol will stain the zinc still further, so that in time, the tables will chart the quaffing sessions of the Chop-house's regulars.

The semi-circular main bar, also zinc-topped, snakes round, leading you on to the restaurant itself beyond the kitchen door and reception area. By the kitchen door stands a marble-topped pastry table stacked high with a robust cornucopia of bread. The table originated from Windsor Castle pastry kitchen and was cut down to size.

To your left, a little alcove leads to the kitchens. Here, the walls are painted with Timna Woollard's mural of choppers, sides of meat, ham, jugs, bowls and sets of scales all abstracted to look faintly like Cornish megaliths in an evocation of Ben Nicholson's paintings. Above the reception desk is a display of meat-cleaver choppers embedded in wood, stern reminders to any customer thinking of not paying. At this point, the main body of the Chop-house dining room stretches out in front of you.

Lining the wall opposite the river is a collection of kitchenware, cooking utensils and china that Conran spent five days arranging on shelves, as in a shop: cheese graters, plates, roasting trays, 'Home Sweet Home' breadboards, gravy jugs, Victorian pewter carving dishes, butter paddles and a Victorian lemon squeezer (Conran's favourite).

When the Chop-house opened, the timbered walls, floor and ceiling looked so new and blond that the interior was more a Butlers Wharf Sauna Cabin than a Chop-house. 'I knew it wasn't right on day one,' says Conran. 'But what could I do? Beat it with chains? Fire guns at it?' The interior has already mellowed into something more along the lines of the pavilion, boathouse or school hall that Conran originally envisaged.

The easy curve of the zinc-topped bar makes an imposing counterpoint to the linear layout of tables and banquettes in the bar area.

The Chop-house chef, Rod Eggleston, the son of school teachers, was born in Cyprus in 1964 and raised in Felsted, Essex. He had always cooked as a hobby but decided to become a chef after taking A levels. He worked two years at Bibendum when it opened in 1987, at Hilaire restaurant in South Kensington, then at the Blue Print Café where he was co-head chef for two years, before moving to the Chop-house.

Like the design, the food at the Chop-house is part traditional British and part 'new' British using traditional ingredients. The recipes that Eggleston has chosen from the Chop-house menu try to reflect this. 'It's taking the best of British food and getting rid of the stodgy overcooked vegetables,' he says. Traditional recipes (see below) are Tomato and Red Leicester Rarebit, Lincolnshire Chine with Mustard Leeks, Fish and Chips with Tartare Sauce, Steak, Kidney and Oyster Pudding, Summer Pudding and Chocolate Sponge with Hot Chocolate Sauce. 'They're simple dishes to make at home which use a number of ingredients that other chefs don't use.'

The wall of kitchenware and cooking utensils creates an effect of homeliness and rusticity. 'What they are saying,' Conran claims, 'is, "Look, this is solid, English-pub-chop-house-dining-room-below-the-stairs taste, and – goodness! – aren't these beautiful objects."'

Views through from the restaurant
to the kitchen remind customers
of the hard work going on behind
the scenes.

Dishes which use traditional ingredients in 'new' ways are Baked Haddock with Parsley and Cheese, Spring Salad with Poached Cod and Lemon Mayonnaise, Turbot and Prawn *en papillote* and Gooseberry and Elderflower Fool.

Most of the recipes, especially Lovage Soup, Baked Haddock and Gooseberry Fool, are easy to make. Spring Salad with Poached Cod is just an assemblage of ingredients. Most popular in the restaurant are Lincolnshire Chine, Steak and Kidney Pudding, Toad in the Hole, Summer Pudding and Gooseberry Fool.

'Most of our meat comes through Smithfield which hangs the meat better than supermarkets,' says Eggleston. 'Our beef is hung from two to three weeks; supermarket beef is probably hung for less than a week, which for our standards isn't long enough. I get pheasant from all over the country, especially Hampshire and Norfolk; grouse from Scotland or Yorkshire; partridge from Yorkshire; venison from the New Forest. I have a guy who dives for scallops and he'll bring them to London twice a week. I have two fishmongers on the coast whom I ring every day. The langoustine fishermen take their catch out of the water to order. I can ring them on their mobile telephones in their boats. Chickens are bought from a free-range farm in Suffolk, which also supplies Lunesdale ducks and free-range turkeys.

While the name 'chop-house' conjures something dark and dingy, this Chop-house is the very antithesis of that: light floods in off the Thames through doors that open on to the riverfront. Outside on the terrace you can sit and eat lunch and dinner, and – at weekends – brunch and delicious cream teas with Chop-house jams. If you look skywards, you'll see teapot spouts which drain rainwater off the glass canopy above you. 'While I was designing this canopy,' recalls Conran, 'I was thinking, "How am I going to get the water away?" when someone brought me a tea tray with a rather good teapot. I thought, "Ah! A teapot spout." This is one of the amusing, slightly quirky details that give me great pleasure.

STARTERS
Lovage Soup
Tomato and Red Leicester Rarebit
Spring Salad with Poached Cod and Lemon Mayonnaise
Baked Haddock with Parsley and Cheese
Lincolnshire Chine with Mustard Leeks
Artichoke with Wild Mushrooms, Poached Egg and Hollandaise

MAIN COURSES
Fish and Chips with Tartare Sauce
Turbot and Prawn En Papillote with Lemon Thyme
Grilled Lobster with Fresh Herbs
Roast Mallard with Seville Orange Sauce
Chicken, Leek and Mushroom Pie
Toad in the Hole with Onion Gravy
Steak, Kidney and Oyster Pudding
Oxtail Faggots with Onion Gravy

DESSERTS
Lemon Syllabub
Lemon Balm Jelly with Summer Fruits
Gooseberry and Elderflower Fool
Summer Pudding
Cherry Eccles Cakes
Chocolate Sponge with Hot Chocolate Sauce

STARTERS

LOVAGE SOUP V

Serves 4

225 g / 8 oz lovage, including stalks
1 large onion, chopped
1 stick celery, chopped
1 small leek, chopped
75 g / 3 oz / 1/3 cup butter
1.2 litres / 2 pints / 5 cups light chicken or vegetable stock
  (see page 136)
Celery salt
White pepper
150 ml / 5 fl oz / 1/2 cup double (heavy) cream, whipped,
  to serve
Croûtons, to serve (see page 138)

Remove the lovage leaves from their stalks. Put the stalks to one side. Place the leaves in a bowl and mash with a fork.

Put the onion, celery, leek and lovage stalks in a saucepan and sweat in the butter until transparent. Add the stock, season with the celery salt and pepper, and bring to the boil. Add the lovage leaves and remove from the heat. Cool and place in the refrigerator.

When chilled, liquidize in a blender or food processor and strain.

Reheat without boiling. Serve hot with cream and croûtons.

TOMATO AND RED LEICESTER RAREBIT V

Serves 4

225 g / 8 oz / 2 cups Red Leicester cheese, grated
3–4 tbsp thick béchamel (see page 137)
2 tsp Worcestershire sauce
2 tbsp Guinness
1 egg yolk
3–4 drops Tabasco sauce
Salt and freshly ground black pepper
4 slices rosemary bread, or bloomer
1 tomato, sliced
1 bunch watercress, to serve

In a bowl mix together the cheese, béchamel, Worcestershire sauce, Guinness, egg yolk and Tabasco. Check the seasoning. Do not add too much béchamel as it will make the topping slide off the toast.

Grill the bread on both sides, and place a slice of tomato on each piece of toast. Cover with the cheese mixture and grill.

Serve garnished with watercress.

SPRING SALAD WITH POACHED COD AND LEMON MAYONNAISE

Serves 4

450 g / 1 lb thick cod, skinned
1 quantity court bouillon (see page 136)
1 lemon, juice and zest
300 ml / 10 fl oz / 1 1/4 cups mayonnaise (see page 137)
100 g / 4 oz mixed salad leaves (could include rocket, lamb's
  lettuce, sorrel, spinach, watercress)
75 g / 3 oz green beans, asparagus tips and fresh peas,
  cooked
50 g / 2 oz / 1/3 cup shallots, chopped
65 ml / 2 1/2 fl oz / 1/4 cup vinaigrette (see page 137)
75 g / 3 oz tomatoes, skinned and seeded

Place the cod in a saucepan, cover with the court bouillon and bring to the boil. Remove from the heat and let the fish go cold in the liquid. When completely cold, remove carefully and separate into large flakes.

To make the lemon mayonnaise, blanch the lemon zest in boiling water and refresh in cold running water. Add the lemon juice and zest to the mayonnaise. Check the seasoning.

To assemble the salad, toss the leaves, beans and shallots with the vinaigrette. Place a pile of the salad in the middle of the plate. Arrange the cod flakes around the edge and top off the salad with the tomato, cut into strips. Serve the mayonnaise separately.

BAKED HADDOCK WITH PARSLEY AND CHEESE

Serves 4

450 g / 1 lb smoked haddock, skinned
450 ml / 15 fl oz / 2 cups double (heavy) cream
2 tbsp parsley, coarsely chopped
50 g / 2 oz / 1/2 cup tomatoes, skinned and very finely diced
Freshly ground black pepper
25–50 g / 1–2 oz / 1/4–1/2 cup Cheddar or Gruyère cheese,
  grated
1–2 tbsp dry breadcrumbs

Place the haddock in a sauté pan and cover with the cream. On a high heat, cook the fish and cream so that the fish flakes and the cream reduces (about 10 minutes).

Remove from the heat, then stir in the parsley and tomatoes. Check the seasoning, divide between four ramekins, then sprinkle with the cheese and breadcrumbs. Place under a grill (broiler) to brown.

Serve with crusty bread and/or salad.

LINCOLNSHIRE CHINE WITH MUSTARD LEEKS

Serves 4

4–5 kg / 8–10 lb boneless neck of pork

Brine
2 tbsp juniper berries
¹/₂ tsp nutmeg
¹/₂ tsp cloves
1 tsp peppercorns
1 large sprig rosemary
3 bay leaves
4.5 litres / 1 gallon / 1¹/₄ US gallons water
550 g / 1¹/₄ lb rock or sea salt
550 g / 1¹/₄ lb caster sugar
2 tbsp saltpetre

Stuffing
4 bunches parsley, finely chopped
1 bunch sage, finely chopped
5 tbsp green peppercorns in brine
¹/₂ tbsp freshly ground black pepper

Mustard Leeks
450 g / 1 lb leeks
100 ml / 3¹/₂ fl oz / ¹/₂ cup olive oil
50 ml / 2 fl oz / ¹/₄ cup vinegar
¹/₂–1 tbsp Dijon mustard
Salt and freshly ground black pepper

Brine
Make a bouquet garni by tying the juniper, nutmeg, cloves, peppercorns, rosemary and bay leaves together with string. Put the water, salt, sugar, saltpetre and bouquet garni in a very large saucepan. Bring slowly to the boil and boil for 3 minutes. Cool.

Remove the skin and trim the fat from the pork. Place in a large stainless steel, plastic or earthenware container, cover with the brine and place a weight on top. The pork should be completely submerged. Refrigerate for five days.

After five days, remove the pork from the brine and stand in a cool, airy place for 24 hours, to drain.

Stuffing
Mix together the parsley, sage, peppercorns and pepper.

Place the pork, skin side down, on a chopping board and make deep cuts in the other side at an angle, along the length, about 4 cm / 1¹/₂ in apart. Do not cut all the way through. Stuff these slashes with the herb mixture, then roll up the pork tightly, tie firmly with string, and wrap in lots of clingfilm. Make sure the clingfilm is tight as this holds the pork's shape. When the meat is sliced, you get the rounds of meat with the herb filling. If the wrapping is too loose, the filling will fall out.

Simmer in a covered pan for 3–3¹/₂ hours. Remember to top up the water with boiling water as necessary.

When cooked, remove the chine, allow to cool and then chill in the refrigerator.

Remove the clingfilm, thinly slice and serve with the mustard leeks.

Mustard Leeks
Cut the leeks into fine slices, blanch in boiling water for 5 minutes and refresh in cold water. Drain.

Combine the olive oil and vinegar into a vinaigrette. Mix the mustard and vinaigrette together and season.

Toss the leeks in the dressing and serve with the chine.

Lincolnshire Chine with Mustard Leeks

S T A R T E R S

ARTICHOKE WITH WILD MUSHROOMS, POACHED EGG AND HOLLANDAISE Ⓥ

Serves 4

3 lemons
4 globe artichokes
1¹/₂ bay leaves
Peppercorns
450 g / 1 lb mixed wild mushrooms
350 g / 12 oz / 1¹/₂ cups unsalted butter
1 garlic clove, chopped
2–3 tbsp parsley, chopped
Salt and freshly ground black pepper
4 egg yolks
3 tbsp vinegar
750 g / 1¹/₂ lb fresh spinach, stems removed
Nutmeg, freshly ground
4 eggs
2–3 tbsp chives, chopped

Fill a bowl with water and add the juice of two lemons. Prepare the artichokes by removing and discarding the outer leaves until you reach the tender parts. As you remove the leaves and the choke place them in the bowl of water to prevent them discolouring.

Put a pan of water on to boil and add half a bay leaf and some peppercorns. Cook the artichokes until soft then refresh with cold water.

Sauté the mushrooms in 50 g / 2 oz / ¹/₄ cup of butter with the garlic for about 5 minutes until soft and juicy. When cooked, add parsley to taste and season. Keep warm.

To make the hollandaise, combine the vinegar, seven peppercorns and a bay leaf in a saucepan and reduce to a tablespoon. Strain into a double boiler, and warm over a gentle heat. Add the egg yolks to the vinegar, stirring all the time. Slowly add 225–250 g / 8–9 oz / 1 cup of butter, piece by piece, whisking all the time. When the sauce is thick, remove from the heat, check the seasoning and add a little lemon juice, to taste. Keep on one side.

Sauté the spinach in 25 g / 1 oz butter with lots of nutmeg. When cooked, check the seasoning and keep warm.

Put a pan of water on to boil and reheat the artichokes. When hot through, drain. Turn the water down to barely a simmer and poach the eggs.

Reheat the mushrooms.

Gently reheat the hollandaise, this must be done carefully as the sauce could curdle.

Pre-heat the grill.

Make a nest of spinach on each plate, top with an artichoke, spoon the wild mushrooms over, and place a poached egg on top. Mask with hollandaise and glaze under the grill. Finally, sprinkle with chives. Delicious with crusty bread.

FISH AND CHIPS WITH TARTARE SAUCE

Serves 4

Batter
10 g / 1/4 oz fresh yeast
1 egg yolk
300–450 ml / 10–15 fl oz / 11/4–2 cups milk, at room
*   temperature*
175 g / 6 oz / 11/4 cups plain flour
100 g / 4 oz / 3/4 cup cornflour
1/2 tsp salt

Chips
1 kg / 2 lb potatoes (Maris Piper, Desirée or other variety
*   suitable for chips)*
2.5–4.5 litres / 6–8 pints / 15–18 cups vegetable oil

Fish
4 x 175–225 g / 6–8 oz pieces plaice, cod or skate, skinned
100 g / 4 oz / 3/4 cup flour, seasoned
2 lemons, cut into wedges
1 bunch watercress

Tartare Sauce
See page 137

Batter
Put the yeast, egg yolk and 300 ml/10 fl oz/11/4 cups of milk in a bowl and mix together. Sift the flour into a separate bowl, and stir in the salt. Beat the milk mixture into the flour, to make a thick dough. Use more milk if the mixture becomes too dense. Cover with a cloth and put in a warm place for 2–3 hours or until it has risen by half.

Chips
Cut the potatoes into thick, square-ended chips. Wash under lots of cold running water and pat dry. Heat the oil to 80°C/180°F, and cook the chips for 6–8 minutes. Drain and remove to one side while you cook the fish.

After frying the fish, cook the chips in the oil at 190°C/375°C until golden. Serve sprinkled with salt.

Fish
Pre-heat the oven to a low temperature (140–150°C/ 275–300°F/gas mark 1–2) to keep the fish warm.

Increase the temperature of the chip oil to 190°C/375°F. Coat the fish with the seasoned flour, and dip in the batter, allowing the excess batter to drip off before placing the fish in the oil. Shake the pan so that the fish pieces do not stick to each other. When golden, drain gently, and place in the oven to keep warm while you cook the chips.

Garnish with watercress and lemon wedges, and serve with tartare sauce.

MAIN COURSES

TURBOT AND PRAWN EN PAPILLOTE WITH LEMON THYME

Serves 4

Prawn Butter
350 g / 12 oz raw prawns
3 tbsp oil
150 ml / 5 fl oz /²⁄₃ cup brandy
1 stick celery, finely chopped
1 carrot, finely chopped
1 small onion, finely chopped
4 dill stalks
1 bay leaf
600 ml / 1 pint / 2¹⁄₂ cups fish stock (see page 136)
1 tbsp tomato paste
Salt and freshly ground black pepper
100 g / 4 oz / ¹⁄₂ cup butter

Turbot
450 g / 1 lb tomatoes, skinned and sliced
1 clove garlic, thinly sliced
Salt and freshly ground black pepper
4 x 175–225 g / 6–8 oz turbot fillets, skinned
1 tbsp lemon thyme

Prawn Butter

Heat the oil in a heavy pan and brown the prawns (still with their shells on), then flambé with the brandy. When the alcohol has burned off, remove the prawns and leave to cool. Add the celery, carrot and onion to the pan and sweat. When the prawns are cool enough to handle, peel and add the shells to the pan. Cook for a few minutes. Add the dill stalks, bay leaf, fish stock and tomato paste and season. Boil to reduce the liquid to a third.

Strain through a fine sieve, pressing hard to get all the flavour out. Return to a clean pan and reduce to six tablespoons. Beat the butter with an electric mixer until light and fluffy. Add the reduced prawn liquid and chill.

Turbot

Pre-heat the oven to 200°C/400°F/gas mark 6. Place a sheet of tin foil, large enough to wrap the fish in, on an oven tray. Put a piece of silicone paper on the bottom of the foil, as this will make it easier to remove the fish when cooked.

Place the tomatoes on the silicone paper, slightly overlapping. Sprinkle the garlic over the tomatoes; season. Sit the turbot fillets on top and sprinkle with the prawns and season again. Arrange the lemon thyme on top. Put two-thirds of the prawn butter over the thyme. Seal the foil tightly. (This can be done the day before, but do not season until just before you put the fish in the oven.) Cook in the oven for 40–45 minutes, or until cooked.

Unwrap the foil and move the fish to a large serving plate. Pour the juices around and serve the remaining butter on the side.

GRILLED LOBSTER WITH FRESH HERBS

Serves 4

4 lobsters, fresh and uncooked
1 clove garlic
1/2 tsp salt
100 g / 4 oz / 1/2 cup butter
4 tbsp white wine
2 tbsp fresh herbs (to include parsley, chervil, tarragon and
  chives), chopped
Freshly ground black pepper
2 lemons, cut in half

Kill the lobster by piercing between the head and body with a heavy sharp knife. Cut in half lengthways with a strong pair of kitchen scissors or shears. Remove the stomach and intestinal tract.

Crust the garlic with the salt using the blade of a large knife. Melt the butter in a large saucepan and cook the garlic until translucent. Add the wine and bring to the boil. Remove from the heat and season.

Grill (broil) the lobster for a few minutes on the shell side. Turn over and when cooked, remove to a serving plate.

Heat the garlic sauce and just before serving stir in the chopped herbs. Check the seasoning. Pour over the lobsters and serve with fresh lemon.

ROAST MALLARD WITH SEVILLE ORANGE SAUCE

Serves 2

4 Seville oranges
1 mallard, plucked and gutted
Dripping
Salt and freshly ground black pepper
1 tbsp redcurrant jelly
250 ml / 8 fl oz / 1 cup dark chicken or game stock
  (see page 136)
1 tbsn butter
Watercress, to serve

Pre-heat the oven to the highest temperature.

Cut one of the oranges into four and stuff inside the bird. Season and seal in the dripping. Place in a roasting tin and cook for 15 minutes until pink, basting the bird at least three times, making sure that you tip the bird so that all the juices run out. Once cooked, remove from the roasting tin and rest in a warm place, breast side down.

To make the sauce, remove the zest from the remaining three oranges, ensuring that none of the white pith remains. Blanch in boiling water for 30 seconds and refresh, then squeeze the juice from the oranges. In a saucepan, heat the redcurrant jelly until it starts to turn from red to brown, then pour in the orange juice. Add the stock and boil, skimming regularly, until the sauce looks like syrup and has a strong flavour. Pass through a fine-mesh sieve into a clean saucepan and whisk in the butter. Keep warm.

Carve the bird in two, adding any juices from it to the sauce. Arrange on a serving dish, add the orange zest to the sauce and pour over the meat. Garnish with sprigs of watercress.

MAIN COURSES

CHICKEN, LEEK AND MUSHROOM PIE

Serves 4

Filling
1 kg / 2 lb legs of corn-fed chicken
Salt and freshly ground black pepper
600 ml / 1 pint / 2½ cups chicken stock (see page 136)
225 g / 8 oz leeks
225 g / 8 oz mixed mushrooms (such as button, oyster, flats, porcini, shitake)
50 g / 2 oz / ¼ cup butter
1–2 tbsp tarragon, chopped
600 ml / 1 pint / 2½ cups double (heavy) cream

Pastry
150 g / 5 oz / ⅔ cup unsalted butter
275 g / 10 oz / 2 cups plain flour
1 tsp salt
3 egg yolks
Iced water
1 egg, beaten

Filling
Pre-heat the oven to 190°C/375°F/gas mark 5.

Season the chicken legs, place on a roasting tray and cook in the oven for 45 minutes, or until roasted. Remove, drain on absorbent paper and cool. Take off all the meat from the bones.

Put the bones and the stock into a saucepan and boil to reduce by half.

Cut the leeks lengthways into quarters then into 2.5 cm/1 in pieces. Blanch in boiling water for 5 minutes and refresh with cold water.

Wash the mushrooms, and cut in half if they are very big. Place them in a sauté pan with the butter and stir until they are cooked and all the liquid has evaporated.

Mix the chicken, leek, mushrooms and tarragon together.

Add the cream to the stock and bones and reduce until thick. Cool, then strain the cream over the chicken mixture. Check the seasoning and pour into a pie dish. Put in the refrigerator to set.

Pastry
Rub the butter into the flour and salt, add the egg yolks and mix to a smooth paste. You might need a little water. Chill for 30 minutes.

To cover the pie, brush the edge of the pie dish with beaten egg and press strips of pastry all round it to make a pastry lip. Roll out the remaining pastry and place on top of the meat so that it is overhanging the pastry lip. Press all round with a fork and trim. Make some leaves or other decorations with the remaining pastry, and attach with beaten egg. Prick the pastry with a fork and brush all over with egg.

Bake in the oven for 30–45 minutes until golden brown.

TOAD IN THE HOLE WITH ONION GRAVY

Serves 4

Toad in the Hole
8 good-quality sausages
4 eggs
300 ml / 10 fl oz / 1¼ cups milk
½ tsp salt
½ tsp pepper
3 tbsp dripping or oil
250 g / 9 oz / 1⅔ cups plain flour, sifted

Onion Gravy
100 g / 4 oz / ½ cup butter
½ carrot, finely diced
1 leek, finely diced
2 sticks celery, finely diced
2 tbsp tomato paste
1 tbsp plain flour
65 ml / 2½ fl oz / ¼ cup Guinness
600 ml / 1 pint / 2½ cups beef stock (see page 136)
2 tbsp redcurrant jelly
4 large onions, sliced
1 tsp English mustard
Salt and freshly ground black pepper

Toad in the Hole
Pre-heat the oven to 190°C/375°F/gas mark 5.

Heat the grill (broiler) and the grill pan with the rack in place. Grill the sausages, making sure that each sausage is evenly cooked, and drain on absorbent paper.

Place the egg, milk and seasoning in a bowl and mix together, then set aside for 15 minutes. Meanwhile, put the dripping or oil in a 1.75 litre/3 pint metal or enamel oven dish, and heat in the oven until smoking. Remove the dish from the oven.

Beat the flour into the egg and milk mixture to form a batter.

Mix the batter and sausages together and place in the heated dish. Put back in the oven and cook for 30–45 minutes, until puffy and golden brown.

Onion Gravy
Melt half the butter in a saucepan and sweat the carrot, leek and celery until transparent. Add the tomato paste and flour, stirring all the time.

Deglaze the pan with the Guinness, making sure everything is combined. Add the stock and redcurrant jelly, bring the mixture to the boil and reduce to 300 ml/10 fl oz/1¼ cup.

Cook the sliced onions in the remaining butter until they are soft and transparent. Strain the gravy on to the onions, add the mustard, and season.

Slice the toad in the hole into generous pieces, arrange on warm plates and spoon the gravy around.

MAIN COURSES

STEAK, KIDNEY AND OYSTER PUDDING

Serves 4

Filling
450 g / 1 lb chuck steak
225 g / 8 oz lambs kidney
100 g / 4 oz / ³/₄ cup flour, seasoned
1 large onion, sliced
300 ml / 10 fl oz / 1¹/₄ cups Guinness
600 ml / 1 pint / 2¹/₂ cups stock (see page 136)
1 bouquet garni
12 oysters (optional)
1 tbsp chives, chopped

Suet Crust
300 g / 11 oz / 2 cups self-raising flour
1 tsp baking powder
Salt and white pepper
¹/₂ tsp thyme leaves, chopped
150 g / 5 oz beef suet
Cold water

Filling
Using a sharp knife, trim the steak of sinew and excess fat and cut into 2.5 cm/1 in pieces. Trim the kidney and cut into 2.5 cm/1 in cubes, removing the core. Sprinkle with seasoned flour and brown, in batches, in a large frying pan. Do not overcrowd the pan. Remove to a large saucepan.

Fry the onion until transparent in the same frying pan.

Deglaze the pan with the Guinness. Add the Guinness and onion mixture, the stock and the bouquet garni to the meat.

Braise for about three hours. Allow to cool and remove any fat from the surface. If the liquor is too thin, strain it off the meat and boil to make it thicker. Reserve about 300 ml/10 fl oz/1¹/₄ cups of liquid for the oysters.

Suet Crust
Mix all the ingredients together in a bowl and add enough cold water to make a firm dough.

Roll out two-thirds of the dough to a thickness of about 5 mm/¹/₄ in. Press this into a large pudding basin, allowing a small overlap at the top. Spoon in the filling. Roll out the remaining dough to the same thickness to fit the top of the basin. Place it on top and pinch around the edge, using the overlap to make a good seal.

Cover the top of the basin with a piece of foil that has a crease folded along the middle. (This will prevent the foil from splitting when the pudding rises.) Tie with string.

Put the basin in a heavy-based pan and add boiling water to the pan to come three-quarters of the way up the sides of the basin. Cover and steam for three hours. Remember not to let the pan boil dry; always top up with boiling water.

Put the oysters in a saucepan with some of the reserved liquid and heat through. Pour over the pudding, and sprinkle with chives.

OXTAIL FAGGOTS WITH ONION GRAVY

Serves 4

Faggots
450 g / 1 lb chuck steak
1 small oxtail
Oil for frying
200 ml / 7 fl oz / 1 cup red wine
2 carrots
2 sticks celery
3 large onions
1 bouquet garni
1 tbsp tomato paste
1 beef stock cube
Salt and freshly ground black pepper
100 g / 4 oz smoked bacon, rind removed
100 g / 4 oz pork fat (unsalted)
100 g / 4 oz calves' liver
2 shallots
1 clove garlic
1 tsp parsley, chopped
1 tsp sage, chopped
50 g / 2 oz / 1/4 cup butter
25 g / 1 oz caul fat

Onion Gravy
See page 113

Using a sharp knife, trim the steak of sinew and excess fat and cut into 2.5 cm/1 in pieces. Trim the oxtail and cut into 2.5 cm/1 in pieces. Brown the oxtail and chuck steak in the oil, drain and remove to a saucepan or casserole.

Deglaze the frying pan with the red wine and pour over the meat. Cut the carrot, celery and one onion into large pieces and add to the meat. Cover with water and add the bouquet garni, tomato paste, stock cube and salt and pepper. Bring to the boil and braise for 3–4 hours, until tender.

When the meat is cooked, remove the vegetables, strain the cooking liquor and allow to cool, then chill in the refrigerator. When cold remove the fat. Boil to reduce to 600 ml/1 pint/2 1/2 cups. Shred the beef and remove the meat from the oxtail, but keep it in chunky pieces.

Mince the bacon, pork fat, liver, shallots and garlic finely. Mix together the bacon mixture, steak, oxtail and add half the parsley and sage. Season.

Cook a little of the meat mixture in a frying pan and taste it to check the flavour. It may need more herbs and seasoning.

Slice the two remaining onions and sweat in the butter. When cooked, add the cooking liquor. Check the seasoning then add to the meat mixture.

Pre-heat the oven to 180°C/350°F/gas mark 4. Shape the meat mixture into eight lozenges then wrap each lozenge shape in caul fat, making sure the overlap is on the bottom of each faggot.

To cook the faggots, place them in a hot dry frying pan, bottom uppermost, and cook until golden brown. Turn over and cook the other side. When all of them are browned, place in the oven to cook through for 15–20 minutes.

Pour some onion gravy on each plate, place two faggots on top and sprinkle with the remaining parsley and sage.

DESSERTS

LEMON SYLLABUB

Serves 4

Syllabub
2 lemons, zest and juice
1 tbsp brandy
300 ml / 10 fl oz / 1¼ cups double (heavy) cream
100 g / 4 oz / ½ cup caster sugar
1 pinch cinnamon

Brandy Snaps
50 g / 2 oz / ¼ cup butter
50 g / 2 oz / ¼ cup sugar
2 tbsp honey
50 g / 2 oz / ⅓ cup plain flour
1 tsp ground ginger
1 tbsp brandy (optional)

Syllabub

Mix together the lemon zest, juice and brandy.
   Whip the cream, sugar and cinnamon until thick.
Slowly whip in the lemon mixture. Pour into wine
glasses and chill overnight.
   Serve with brandy snaps.

Brandy Snaps

Pre-heat the oven to 180°C/350°F/gas mark 4.
   Put the butter, sugar and honey into a saucepan and
melt over a low heat. Stir to dissolve the sugar. Remove
from the heat and sift in the flour and ground ginger.
Mix together. Add the brandy, if desired.
   Grease an oven tray, and the handles of several wooden
spoons, with butter. Drop large spoonfuls of the mixture
onto the tray, separated by spaces of about 7.5 cm/3 in,
as they will spread during cooking. Bake for 5–10
minutes, until golden.

Remove the tray from the oven and allow to stand for
2 minutes. Use an egg slice or spatula to remove each
brandy snap, then wrap it around the handle of a
wooden spoon. When crisp, slide off and put on a wire
rack to cool.

LEMON BALM JELLY WITH SUMMER FRUITS

Serves 4

225 g / 8 oz / 1 cup caster sugar
450 ml / 15 fl oz / 2 cups water
25 g / 1 oz lemon balm
1 bottle Sauterne
3½ tbsp gelatine
1 lemon, juiced
Summer fruits (to include blueberry, peach, melon, passion
   fruit, kiwi)

Bring the sugar and water to the boil and boil for 5
minutes. Remove from the heat and pour off 85 ml/
3 fl oz/⅓ cup. Infuse the lemon balm in the remaining
syrup until cold.
   Strain the lemon-balm syrup, measure it and add
enough Sauterne to make 600 ml/1 pint/2½ cups.
   Warm 50 ml/2 fl oz/¼ cup of Sauterne and dissolve the
gelatine in it. Mix the lemon-balm syrup, gelatine and
lemon juice, check the sweetness and add more sugar if
needed. Pour into four 200 ml/7 fl oz/1 cup dariole
moulds and chill overnight.
   Prepare the summer fruits, mix with the remaining
syrup, and add a little Sauterne.
   Turn the jellies out and serve with fruit salad on the
side.

GOOSEBERRY AND ELDERFLOWER FOOL

Serves 4

1 kg / 2 lb / 7 cups gooseberries
100 g / 4 oz / ¹⁄₂ cup caster sugar
65 ml / 2¹⁄₂ fl oz / ¹⁄₄ cup elderflower cordial
300 ml / 10 fl oz / 1¹⁄₄ cups double (heavy) cream
Langues de chat biscuits, to serve

In a saucepan stew the gooseberries with the sugar, cordial and a little water, until soft. Cool. Liquidize in a blender or food processor and sieve. Check the sweetness and add more cordial if needed. Chill.

Softly whip the cream and fold into the purée. Pour into individual glasses and chill.

Serve decorated with elderflowers and *Langues de chat*.

SUMMER PUDDING

Serves 4

1.25 kg / 2¹⁄₂ lb / 8¹⁄₂ cups mixed red berries (redcurrants, raspberries, strawberries, cherries)
200 ml / 7 fl oz / ³⁄₄ cup water
175 g / 6 oz / 1 cup caster sugar
10 slices medium-sliced white bread, preferably one day old
Clotted cream, to serve

Place 1 kg/2 lb/7 cups of the summer fruit (except the strawberries) in a saucepan, add the water and sprinkle the sugar over. Bring to the boil and simmer for 2–3 minutes. Remove from the heat. Check the sweetness and add more sugar if necessary. If using strawberries and they are very large, cut them into smaller pieces. Add the strawberries to the rest of the fruit mixture.

Strain the fruit and keep the juice. Remove the crusts

Cherry Eccles Cake

from the bread and line the pudding basin with the slices, dipping them in to fruit juice as you go. Place the fruit in the bread-lined basin and cover with a lid of bread.

Cover with clingfilm, place a small tea plate on top and put some heavy weights on the plate to squeeze out the juices. Chill overnight, turn out and spoon over with some of the reserved juice. Garnish the remaining fresh fruit and serve with clotted cream.

CHERRY ECCLES CAKES

Serves 4

450 g / 1 lb / 3¹/₂ cups cherries
150 ml / 5 fl oz / ²/₃ cup water
100 g / 4 oz / ¹/₂ cup caster sugar
450 g / 1 lb puff pastry (see page 141)
50 g / 2 oz / ¹/₃ cup plain flour
1 egg, beaten
2 tbsp water
1¹/₂ tbsp caster sugar
Clotted cream, to serve

Pre-heat the oven to 200°C/400°F/gas mark 6.

Poach the cherries in the water and half the sugar until cooked, but still firm. Drain and cool.

Roll out the puff pastry to a thickness of about 3 mm/¹/₈ in and cut out four 15 cm/6 in circles.

Toss the cherries with the plain flour and a little sugar, if needed. Put a pile of cherries in the middle of each pastry circle. Brush with beaten egg, pull the edge together and seal in the centre. Turn over and press down. Score the top three times.

Place on an oven tray lined with silicone paper and brush with a glaze, made with the water and caster sugar. Bake for about 20 minutes until golden brown.

Serve with clotted cream.

CHOCOLATE SPONGE WITH HOT CHOCOLATE SAUCE

Serves 4

Sponge
75 g / 3 oz dark chocolate
100 g / 4 oz / ¹/₂ cup butter
100 g / 4 oz / ¹/₂ cup caster sugar
2 eggs
100 g / 4 oz / ³/₄ cup plain flour, sifted
¹/₂ tsp baking powder
2 tbsp milk

Sauce
100 g / 4 oz dark chocolate
50 ml / 2 fl oz / ¹/₄ cup milk
2 egg yolks
50 g / 2 oz / ¹/₄ cup caster sugar
25 g / 1 oz / ¹/₈ cup unsalted butter

Sponge

Pre-heat the oven to 160°C/325°F/gas mark 3.

Melt the chocolate in a double-boiler until soft. Cream together the butter and sugar in a mixing bowl, and gradually add the eggs. Beat in the flour and baking powder and finally the chocolate and milk.

Divide the mixture between four 200 ml/7 fl oz/1 cup metal moulds and bake in the oven for 20–30 minutes, until risen and cooked through. Rest a few minutes before turning out.

Sauce

Melt the chocolate in the milk. Add the egg yolks and sugar and cook gently, stirring all the time until thick. Just before serving, whisk in the butter.

THE SHOPS

'It wouldn't be the **Gastrodrome** without them'
Sir Terence Conran

A view of the Gastrodrome looking along Shad Thames.

Imagine a village in Europe whose inhabitants take food and drink so seriously that any shop not selling these goods is excluded. That's the idea behind the Gastrodrome shops.

There are five shops in this food-oriented village: the Food Store, Smoked Fish and Crustacea Shop, the Oils and Spices Shop the Chop-house Shop and the Wine Merchant. They operate as satellite operations nestling in the nooks and crannies of the 'mother' ships of Le Pont de la Tour and the Butlers Wharf Chop-house.

'To try and explain what I wanted to do,' says Conran, 'I showed everyone photographs of small specialist shops in France, Italy and Spain. We even sent the manageress of the shops to Paris with a list of suitable delicatessens to visit.'

On their own, the shops probably wouldn't work, although each one contributes 'a small profit'. 'If one was being rational,' adds Conran, 'they probably wouldn't be there. But it wouldn't be the Gastrodrome without them. I was trying to create an area of activity where everything has synergy.'

Buff paper carrier bags, Le Pont de la Tour wrapping paper and an absence of plastic under-line the earnestness of the endeavour. Since the goods sold in the shops are the same as those supplied to Le Pont de la Tour's kitchen, any fresh food left unsold at the end of the day goes straight to the head chef, David Burke, for use that evening. The shops may be economically indulgent, but they are not wasteful.

Branding of the Gastrodrome extends to brown paper carriers.

All the ingredients for the 'Basic' recipes (see page 135) can be bought at the Gastrodrome.

The Food Store

'The Food Store is the Butlers Wharf community shop,' says Conran. 'Since there's a Safeway and Tesco nearby, there's no point in trying to compete with them, so the idea was to create a delicatessen selling daily bread baked by our own bakery and specialist items that people in this area might like.'

With the dimensions of an upended shoe box situated next to the entrance of Le Pont de la Tour, the Food Store looks like a Victorian corner shop crossed with a Milanese delicatessen: chequered blue-and-white tile floor, huge wall-clock, a counter with cold meats and cheeses, racks of freshly baked bread, strings of bulbous onions and garlic hanging in the windows, and shelves crammed with pastas, coffee, rice, chocolate, biscuits, jars of pickled this and preserved that. Reaching up to the soaring two-storey-tall ceiling is a museum of old-fashioned branded cardboard packing cases, some of which are empty and just for show.

'We were left with this tiny space,' explains Conran, 'so I've given it a feeling of something very, very high, so that when people walk in they get a surprise. In the back of my memory is lodged a place in southern Italy where I went into a shop that was enormously high and seemed to be coloured yellow and turquoise with shelves reaching up and things hanging down. The big clock is something you might find in a little corner shop in Italy or France. It seems to go with the height of the room.'

There's an Italian accent to many of the goods: salamis, prosciutto, De Cecco pasta (Italy's bestseller), Cipriani pasta (egg tagliardi, tagliolini and tagliatelle) and Calabrian sun-dried tomatoes. Pains are taken to source everything properly, usually by asking the embassy of the source country for lists of importers.

Owing to lack of space, only bestselling cheeses are stocked: Parmesan, Brie,

The Food Store is a tiny space enticingly packed with the best produce.

Stilton, English goat's cheese from Gedi in Barnet and Cheddar from Neal's Yard. Cashel Blue soft Irish cheese was added after customers kept marching in from Le Pont de la Tour, where it appears on the cheeseboard, and asking to buy some to take home.

Fruit and vegetables spilling from crates outside the shop are of the same type and range as supplied to Le Pont de la Tour: Provençal vegetables, aubergines, peppers, French beans, courgettes, squash, custard marrows and chilli peppers supplied by Conran's personal potager in Berkshire.

What really flies out of the Food Store are the fresh breads baked daily next door in the Gastrodrome Bakery. The Bakery opened at the same time as Le Pont de la Tour and the Food Store in 1991. It is not a shop, but a proper working bakery that supplies most of the Gastrodrome's needs, firing up at 4 am and working through to noon. Run by Neville Wilkins, it bakes about 250 loaves a day in up to fifty varieties from basic French baguettes via pain de campagne and granary bread to breads with a wide range of added ingredients such as sun-dried tomato, spinach and nutmeg, cumin and ceps. Most popular are ciabatta, Italian walnut and date, sun-dried tomato, olive, and onion and bacon. Because space is so limited, the Bakery's schedule is pared down to produce exactly what the Gastrodrome needs, but in the future Conran hopes to expand the bread-making activities.

The Food Store is open from Monday to Friday, from 10 am to 8.30 pm, and at weekends from 10 am to 6 pm.

The Smoked Fish and Crustacea Shop

Tiled floors and walls lend an air of cleanliness and simplicity to the Smoked Fish and Crustacea Shop. The foreground of the shop is now packed with an abundant stock of fresh flowers.

The sight of salted dried cod and tuna dangling upside down from the ceiling looking utterly astonished at being dead greets you as you enter this small shop at the downstream end of the Butlers Wharf Building, behind Cantina del Ponte.

To your left is a counter crammed with a fresh seafood anthology heaped up with meticulous insouciance on crushed ice. To your right stands a row of

Dried salted fish hang inside the entrance to the Smoked Fish and Crustacea Shop.

earthenware bowls filled with preserved, pickled and marinated fish and seafoods: herrings in mustard sauce are especially popular, followed by *insalata di mare* from Loch Fyne, the seafood specialists. Dried, tinned and bottled sardines, anchovies, mussels and squid from Spain and Italy are stacked on shelves around your head.

The Smoked Fish and Crustacea Shop was inspired by a visit Conran made to Loch Fyne in Argyll which supplies kippers, Finnan haddock and whole eel. The shop's mainstays are Irish salmon lightly smoked over beech as used in Le Pont de la Tour; Loch Fyne salmon, smoked over old oak whisky barrels to give a medium smoke; and English salmon fumed over oak logs by Minola in Gloucestershire to give a heavy smoke. With the exception of kippers, haddock and cold-smoked fish, all fish stocked is ready to eat. The shop does not stock wet fish unless requested. Eel fillets, trout, bloaters and buckling are either hot-smoked (ready to eat) or cold-smoked (still needing cooking). The shop also sells cod's roe, gravadlax, Arbroath smokies and smoked mackerel.

The range of crustacea is the same as at the Crustacea Bar in the entrance hall of Le Pont de la Tour: crab, lobster, Irish oysters (rock and, when in season, native), clams, mussels, scallops, langoustines and whole *plateaux de fruits de mer* (including wire stand) to take away. The majority of crustacea come from Scotland and Dorset except lobsters which are sometimes flown in from Canada.

A mouth-watering array of food tempts the tastebuds.

The Smoked Fish and Crustacea Shop also sells bagels filled with salmon and cream cheese, gravadlax with dill mustard sauce or smoked trout fillets with horseradish. Freshly prepared soup of the day is supplied daily by Le Pont de la Tour. Olives, pickles, gherkins and capers are widely praised, and the shop sells the black and green herbed variety of olives served in Le Pont de la Tour. Spanish green olives are stuffed with anchovies and marinated in oil, chillies, garlic and lemon.

Curiously, the biggest seller is not fish, or even food. What makes the tills ring are fresh flowers from New Covent Garden Market. On Conran's instructions, carnations, dried grasses and pom-pom chrysanthemums are banned.

The Smoked Fish and Crustacea Shop is open from Monday to Friday, noon to 8.30 pm, and at weekends from 10 am to 6 pm.

Staff are on hand to advise any customers bewildered by the sheer range of olive oils and spices on sale.

The Oils and Spices Shop

Follow your nose and you can't fail to find this nook behind the Butlers Wharf Chop-house. Spices were ground at Butlers Wharf for 150 years before Butlers, Grinders & Operators moved out in 1994. Conran has revived the tradition in miniature. The Oils and Spices Shop sells fifty spices, the full list of which reads like an Oriental Rabelais in full flow (galangal, garam masala, karali masala . . .). Most popular are cinnamon, ginger and allspice, but you can order any spice under the sun. Japanese customers buy peppercorns by the sackful; they're ten times more expensive in Japan. Most spices arrive whole and are ground to order.

This is oil heaven, too. The fifty or so olive oils from all over the world span the full spectrum of flavours: spicy, buttery, herby, soft and avocado-like, 'tomato skin', bitter chocolate, burnt almond, fresh crisp green banana.

Traditional Mediterranean countries are well represented. Israel gets a mention with Canaan oil. Even Australia provides three notable oils from Joseph, Foothills and Viva. Bestsellers are dell'Ugo from Italy, Nuñez de Prado from Spain, La Rosa from Portugal, oil from Mausanne and Fontvielle co-ops and olives from Mas de Brunelys, Conran's *propriété* in Provence.

There are also nut oils, seed oils and lemon oils – all used in Le Pont de la Tour – herb oils, chilli oils, spiced basting oils and general commercial olive oils. Of the flavoured oils, basil and lemon are most popular. You can also buy balsamic vinegars and mustards.

Fresh herbs come in two types: potted and cut. In summer, potted basil, thyme, sage and parsley come from Conran's herb garden. Dried herbs and spices are bought whole or ground, by weight.

Any thwarted chemist would have great fun here because the Oils and Spices Shop also stocks endless accessories: empty bottles, oil cans, pepper grinders, oil pourers, storage tins and labels, seven-litre glass robinets and a range of cook-books.

The Oils and Spices Shop is open from Monday to Friday, noon to 6 pm, and at weekends from 10 am to 6 pm.

The Chop-house Shop

Sometimes referred to as the Chop Shop, the Chop-house Shop is the Butlers Wharf butcher, pie-maker, game-dealer and dessert pudding-maker rolled into one tiny stall in the entrance of the Butlers Wharf Chop-house. Its oaken fittings and fixtures continue the Chop-house's theme of solid modern Englishness. In height it is similar to the Food Store, but the upper reaches of the walls have ash slats, like a huge Venetian blind, which hide the offices on the first floor of this part of the Butlers Wharf Building.

To one side is a counter and kitchen range manned by a couple of aproned chefs; opposite stands an oak-trimmed chest fridge with meats, fowls, pies and home-made sausages from the Chop-house kitchen. Shelves are stocked with pickles, chutneys and jams also made in the restaurant kitchen. Here you can buy the basic meats for all the recipes in this book and more besides: rib steaks, sirloin, fillet, corn-fed chicken, lamb and veal chops, guinea fowl, home-made sausages (including beef and coriander, venison and cranberry, veal and lemon, port and tarragon, duck and orange), pies, faggots, black pudding, duck, lamb's kidneys, calves' liver, wood pigeon, grouse and partridge. Big movers are steak and kidney pies, chicken, leek and mushroom pies, sausages, steak, chicken and chops. At lunchtime, you can buy hot roast beef sandwiches, bacon sandwiches, hot sausages and home-made soup from the Chop-house Shop.

The Chop-house Shop is open from Monday to Friday, noon to 8 pm, and at weekends from noon to 6 pm.

The Wine Merchant

The Wine Merchant buys, stores and supplies wines for the entire Gastrodrome. It is located at the downstream end of Butlers Wharf Building (next to the Smoked Fish and Crustacea Shop) and is accessible from both Shad Thames and from the far end of Le Pont de la Tour. Its cavernous interior, stone-flagged floor, vaulted ribbed-wood ceiling and subdued lighting give the feel of a wine cellar.

The Wine Merchant handles wine from all over the world, tailored to the lists of Le Pont de la Tour, the Chop-house, Cantina del Ponte and the Blue Print Café. Wines are bought to suit the style of each restaurant. Le Pont de la Tour's 900-bottle list concentrates on Bordeauxs, Burgundy, fine wines and top wines from the New World. Because of its breadth, the other restaurants can feed off existing Pont lines, but with the addition of specific wines brought in specifically for each restaurant,

they can still maintain a uniqueness and individuality.

The Chop-house's list of 180 wines feeds off certain stock from Le Pont, but it also holds its own exclusive wines: Henschke Cabernet Shiraz from Australia, Meerlust Merlot from South Africa and Ridge Chardonnay from North America. It concentrates on classic Bordeaux and big meaty voluptuous wines that go well with a variety of rustic meat dishes. 'The Chop-house was a problem,' says Conran, referring to the lack of decent English wines. 'We thought of having wines from our old colonies, but ended up concentrating on claret in jugs and a good port list – quite British in its way.'

When Cantina del Ponte first opened, its wine list was 80 per cent Italian. The remainder came from other Mediterranean countries, but this proved unsatisfactory. Now the list is all-Italian and covers the whole of the Italian boot from top to toe, including varieties like white Pomino from Frescobaldi, a white blend or pinot bianco and chardonnay, and one of a handful of whites to be produced in the predominantly red Chianti region of Tuscany. Close by is the Chianti Rufina from Selvapiano, and then further afield, Salice Salentino from Puglia. Deep in the heel of southern Italy, Puglia is not a vast wine-producing region, but Francesco Candido's oak-aged Salice is extremely impressive.

The menu at the Blue Print Café calls for light, lively wines from Australia, New Zealand, South and North America and South Africa, such as Firebreak Sangiovese from Shafer in the Napa Valley in Utah, and a top-notch Sauvignon known as 'The Arts' series from Leeuwin Estate in Western Australia.

The Wine Merchant's buyers are forever searching out new wines, and introducing them to the Gastrodrome sommeliers. 'Customers are becoming more educated and knowledgeable,' they say, 'but it can be disheartening to see excellent but unusual wines gathering dust, while the more established names such as Chablis, Pouilly-Fumé and Sancerre continue to dominate the market.'

The idea of opening the Wine Merchant directly on to Le Pont de la Tour is partly to enable sommeliers to retrieve wines from the racks, but also to inspire customers to decant themselves on to the trestle table and finish off their dinner over Armagnacs and Cognacs. 'I got the idea from the Operakelln in Stockholm and from Tour d'Argent in Paris,' says Conran. 'After dinner you adjourn to the cellar. I'm disappointed it's not used more often.'

The Wine Merchant is open from Monday to Saturday, noon to 8.30 pm, and on Sunday from noon to 3 pm.

The Wine Merchant acts as a cellar for all the restaurants as well as a fabulously stocked off-license for the wine connoisseur. The vaulted ceiling gives something of the feeling of a traditional vintner's cellar.

BASIC RECIPES

STOCKS, SAUCES AND ACCOMPANIMENTS

FISH STOCK

Makes 1 litre/1³/₄ pints/4 cups

1–2 lb / 450 g–1 kg fish bones and trimmings
1 large onion, coarsely chopped
2 large carrots
3 sticks celery
1 whole mace
10 peppercorns
2 bay leaves
1 lemon, cut into quarters
2 cloves
2 tbsp parsley stalks
2.75 litres / 5 pints / 12 cups water

Put all the ingredients into a saucepan and bring to the boil. Turn down and simmer until reduced by a third. Strain, return to a clean pan and reduce by half.
  Use as required.

MEAT STOCK

Makes 1.5 litres/2¹/₂ pints/6¹/₄ .cups

1 kg / 2 lb bones
275 g / 10 oz vegetables (to include onion, carrot, celery leek), sliced
100 g / 4 oz bacon rind
50 g / 2 oz mushroom peelings
1 handful parsley stalks
1 bouquet garni
1 tsp salt
5 peppercorns
2.25–2.75 litres / 4–5 pints / 10–12 cups water, or to cover

Use bones for a specific stock, that is veal, beef, lamb, chicken, and so on.
  Pre-heat the oven to 220°C/425°F/gas mark 7.
  Brown the bones and vegetables in a hot oven. Put the bones, bacon rind, vegetables, mushroom peelings, parsley, bouquet garni, salt and peppercorns into a large saucepan and cover with water.
  Bring slowly to the boil, skim and simmer gently for 3–4 hours. Strain and cool. When cold, remove the fat.
  Put into a clean pan and reduce by half. Check seasoning and use as required.

COURT BOUILLON

Makes 1 litre/1³/₄ pints/4 cups

900 ml / 1¹/₂ pints / 3¹/₂ cups water
150 ml / 5 fl oz / ²/₃ cup white wine
3 tbsp white wine vinegar
12 peppercorns
2 bay leaves
1 large piece mace
2 cloves
¹/₂ leek, diced
1 carrot, diced
3 shallots, diced
1 celery stick, diced
1 handful of parsley stalks
1 lemon, cut into quarters

Put all the ingredients into a saucepan and bring to the boil.
  Boil for 20 minutes and strain. Use as required.

BÉCHAMEL

Makes 450 ml/15 fl oz/2 cups

1 small onion, cut in half
1 bay leaf
8–10 peppercorns
2 cloves
1 piece mace
450 ml / 15 fl oz / 2 cups milk
50 g / 2 oz / 1/4 cup butter
50 g / 2 oz / 1/3 cup flour

Put the onion, bay leaf, peppercorns, cloves and mace in the milk. Heat gently, and leave to infuse for a couple of hours.

Melt the butter over a medium heat, add the flour and make a roux. Strain the milk over the roux, stirring all the time, and cook until thick. Check the seasoning.

Use as required.

VINAIGRETTE

Makes 1.25 litres/2¼ pints/5 cups

2 tbsp Dijon mustard
65 ml / 2½ fl oz / 1/4 cup red wine vinegar
150 ml / 5 fl oz / 2/3 cup water
2 tbsp sherry vinegar
300 ml / 10 fl oz / 1¼ cups peanut oil
150 ml / 5 fl oz / 2/3 cup walnut oil
900 ml / 1½ pints / 3½ cups olive oil
1 tsp salt
1 tsp pepper

Combine all the ingredients in a clean glass container and store in the refrigerator. Mix well before use.

MAYONNAISE

Makes 300 ml/10 fl oz/1¼ cups

3 egg yolks
Salt and freshly ground black pepper
1–2 tsp Dijon mustard
1–2 tbsp white wine vinegar
300 ml / 10 fl oz / 1¼ cups olive oil or vegetable oil

By hand or using a food processor with metal blades, beat the egg yolks with two large pinches of salt, until pale. Beat in a teaspoon mustard and a few grinds of pepper.

Very slowly, dribble the oil into the yolk mixture, beating all the time. When half the oil is incorporated, add a tablespoon of vinegar.

Beat in the rest of the oil and check the seasoning. You may need to add a little more vinegar or mustard.

The mayonnaise will keep in the refrigerator for a few days.

TARTARE SAUCE

Serves 4

300 ml / 10 fl oz / 1¼ cups mayonnaise
50 g / 2 oz gherkins, finely chopped
50 g / 2 oz capers, chopped
1½ tbsp parsley, chopped
1½ tbsp tarragon
Salt and freshly ground black pepper

Mix together all the ingredients and add the pepper. Check before adding salt, as you may not need too much.

The tartare sauce will keep in the refrigerator for a few days. Ideal for any fried or grilled fish.

DILL SAUCE

Serves 4

150 ml / 5 fl oz / ²/₃ cup mayonnaise
3 tsp coarse mustard
2 tbsp dill, chopped
1 tsp sugar
Salt and freshly ground black pepper

Mix all the ingredients together, and serve with smoked fish.

The sauce will keep in the refrigerator for a few days.

ROUILLE

Serves 4

3 hot red chillies, seeded and chopped
4 garlic cloves, chopped
1 large red pepper, skinned, seeded and chopped
3 egg yolks
300 ml / 10 fl oz / 1¹/₄ cups olive oil
Salt and freshly ground black pepper

Mix the chillies, garlic and pepper in a food processor. When smooth, add the egg yolks one at a time, mixing between each. Very slowly dribble in the olive oil, as if making mayonnaise. Add salt and pepper to taste.

This will keep for 2–3 days in the refrigerator. As well as being a traditional soup accompaniment, it can be used on potatoes and salads and as a dip.

CROÛTONS

Serves 4

3 slices white bread, medium thick
600 ml / 1 pint / 2¹/₂ cups vegetable oil

Remove the crusts and cut the bread into cubes. Heat the oil and fry the cubes until golden. Drain on kitchen paper.

Perfect for soups and salads.

SUN-DRIED TOMATO PESTO

Serves 4

75 g / 3 oz sun-dried tomatoes, in oil
2 cloves garlic, coarsely chopped
50 g / 2 oz / ¹/₂ cup pine nuts
300 ml / 10 fl oz / 1¹/₄ cups good-quality olive oil
50 g / 2 oz / ¹/₂ cup Parmesan cheese, grated
¹/₄ tsp salt
¹/₄ tsp black pepper

Drain the sun-dried tomatoes, then place in a food processor with the garlic and mix for 30 seconds. Add the pine nuts and half the olive oil, and mix for another 30 seconds. Add the Parmesan, remaining oil and seasoning, and mix until smooth.

Keep in a jar in the refrigerator for up to 2 weeks. Make sure there is a film of oil covering the pesto as this acts as a seal.

PESTO

Serves 4

75 g / 3 oz / 1 cup basil leaves
2 cloves garlic, coarsely chopped
50 g / 2 oz / 1/2 cup pine nuts
300 ml / 10 fl oz / 1 1/4 cups good-quality olive oil
50 g / 2 oz / 1/2 cup Parmesan cheese, grated
1/4 tsp salt
1/4 tsp black pepper

Combine, as for Sun-dried Tomato Pesto (see above), starting with the basil leaves and garlic. Store as above.

Flavoured oils and vinegars make wonderful salad dressings and mayonnaise and sauces that incorporate them can take on a new lease of life.

   Making flavoured oils and vinegars is very simple, and the combinations of flavourings are endless. Here are a few points to remember.

1. Make sure the bottles are clean and dry.
2. If using fresh herbs, make sure the leaves are unblemished. Wash and dry then before placing in the liquid. Lightly bruise the leaves to help release the flavour.
3. When using ingredients such as ginger and chillies, encourage them to release more flavour. Peel the ginger and cut into attractive shapes; prick chillies a few times with a pin.
4. White wine vinegar is usually used for flavouring but you can use other types. Combine the ingredients with the vinegar in a saucepan, and warm over a gentle heat. Allow to cool then bottle and cap tightly. Leave in a sunny place for 2–3 weeks, then strain and rebottle. Store in a cool, dark place.

5. Most flavoured oils use olive oil as a base, but there are many other types that can make interesting combinations. Oils do not need straining, but they do need to infuse for 2–3 weeks before using.

CHAMP

Serves 4

1 kg / 2 lb baking potatoes, peeled
225 g / 8 oz spring onions
300 ml / 10 fl oz / 1 1/4 cups milk
100 g / 4 oz / 1/2 cup butter
Salt and freshly ground black pepper

Dice the potatoes, place in a pan of cold water and bring to the boil. Cook until soft, then drain.

   Slice the spring onions, including most of the green part then infuse in the milk over a low heat.

   Dry the cooked potatoes on the stove, then mash until completely smooth.

   Add the spring onions, some of the milk and the butter. Mix well, adding milk as necessary. Season. The champ should have a nice creamy texture.

COLCANNON

Serves 4

1 kg / 2 lb baking potatoes, peeled
450 g / 1 lb cabbage, sliced
1 medium Spanish onion, finely chopped
225 g / 8 oz / 1 cup butter
Salt and freshly ground black pepper

Dice the potatoes, place in a pan of cold water and bring to the boil. Cook until soft, then drain.

Fry the cabbage and onion in half the butter until soft, but do not allow them to colour.

Dry the potatoes on the stove and mash until smooth.

Add the cooked cabbage and onion to the potatoes then mix in the rest of the butter. Season and serve.

BREADS AND PASTRIES

BLINIS

Makes 12 x 10 cm / 4 in blinis

10 g / ¼ oz fresh yeast
½ tsp sugar
100 g / 4 oz / ¾ cup buckwheat flour
150 ml / 5 fl oz / ⅔ cup milk mixed with 150 ml / 5 fl oz /
⅔ cup water
75 g / 3 oz / ½ cup plain flour
1 large egg, separated
1 tbsp butter
½ tsp salt
150 ml / 5 fl oz / ⅔ cup milk
Caviare, smoked salmon and crème fraîche, to serve

Cream the yeast and sugar together, then mix with the buckwheat flour. Warm the water/milk and add to the buckwheat mixture until you have a thick cream. Leave in a warm place to rise for 20–30 minutes.

In a separate bowl, mix the plain flour, egg yolk, butter, salt and milk until you have a thick batter.

When the buckwheat has risen, fold it into the plain flour batter. Cover with a cloth, put in a warm place and leave to rise for 2 hours.

When it is time to cook the blinis, whip the egg white until it forms soft peaks. Fold this into the blini mix.

Heat a heavy, cast-iron pancake pan and grease with a little butter. When the pan is hot, pour in a tablespoon of batter. When bubbles appear on the upper side and the bottom lifts easily, it is time to flip the blini over. When both sides are cooked, keep warm in the bottom of the oven, covered with loose foil.

Serve with caviare, smoked salmon and crème fraîche.

FOCACCIA

Serves 4–6

½ tsp fresh yeast
1 tsp sugar
150 ml / 5 fl oz / ⅔ cup warm water
450 g / 1 lb / 3 cups strong plain flour
85 ml / 3 fl oz / ⅓ cup olive oil
2 egg yolks
1 tsp salt
Olive oil, for dribbling over
Sea salt

Dissolve the yeast and sugar in the warm water. Sieve the plain flour into a large bowl, make a well in the centre and add the yeast and sugar solution, olive oil, egg yolks and salt. With your hands, mix to a pliable dough and knead well for about 10 minutes. Place in a clean bowl, cover with a cloth and leave to rise for 2–2¹/₂ hours. Knead for another 10 minutes. Press the dough with one finger to form well-spaced craters.

Put the dough into a greased 30 cm/12 in square tin, and flatten so that it fills the tin evenly. Dribble olive oil over and sprinkle with sea salt. Rest for 1–2 hours.

Pre-heat the oven to 190°C/375°F/gas mark 5. Bake for 20–30 minutes, or until golden brown.

BRIOCHE

Makes 3 loaves

25 g / 1 oz fresh yeast
100 ml / 3¹/₂ fl oz / ¹/₂ cup milk, at room temperature
1 kg / 2 lb 4 oz / 7 cups strong plain flour
12 eggs
65 g / 2¹/₂ oz caster sugar
25 g / 1 oz salt
550 g / 1 lb 4 oz / 2¹/₂ cups unsalted butter, at room
  temperature
1 egg, for glazing

Dissolve the yeast in the milk and then add to the flour. In a food mixer, beat with a dough hook for ten minutes on medium speed.

In a separate bowl mix together the sugar, salt and eggs, stirring constantly until the sugar has dissolved. Add this mixture to the dough and mix.

Cut the butter into cubes and add to the dough. When thoroughly mixed, put into a clean bowl, cover with a cloth and leave for 2–3 hours or until it has doubled in size.

Remove the dough and knead. Put back into the bowl and rest for 1–2 hours.

Remove from the bowl, shape into lozenges and put into three 1 kg/2 lb greased loaf tins. Leave to rise again for another 1–2 hours.

Pre-heat the oven to 190°C/375°F/gas mark 5.

Before baking, brush with beaten egg and bake for 15 minutes, then reduce heat to 160°C/325°F/gas mark 3 for 10 minutes. Remove from the oven, tap the bottom of the loaf – it will make a hollow sound when it is ready.

PUFF PASTRY

Serves 4

450 g / 1 lb / 2 cups unsalted butter
450 g / 1 lb / 3 cups plain flour, sifted
¹/₂ tsp salt
Iced water
¹/₂ lemon, juiced

Cut the butter into 2.5 cm/1 in cubes.

Place the flour and salt in a bowl, add the iced water and lemon juice, and work together with your fingertips until it is a firm dough.

Roll the dough out to a rectangle about 1 cm/¹/₂ in thick. Dot one half with the cubes of butter leaving an edge 2.5 cm/1 in wide all round. Fold the points of the pastry over and gently press down the edges. Set aside for about 10 minutes.

With the folded end facing away from you, roll the dough out into a rectangle and fold in three. Roll out again and fold. Do this process four more times, chilling between each roll and fold.

Chill before using as required.

SWEET PASTRY

Makes enough for 2 x 20 cm/8 in loose-bottom flan tins or 8 individual 11 cm/4^{1}/$_{2}$ in fluted flan tins

225 g/8 oz/1^{1}/$_{2}$ cups plain flour, sifted
120 g/4^{1}/$_{2}$ oz/1^{1}/$_{2}$ cup icing sugar
1 pinch of salt
120 g/4^{1}/$_{2}$ oz/1^{1}/$_{2}$ cup unsalted butter, chilled
2 egg yolks
Cold milk

Using a wooden spoon, combine the flour, icing sugar and salt in a mixing bowl, and rub in the butter.
  Mix in the egg yolks to make a good dough consistency. Add milk if necessary. This is a very delicate pastry.
  Chill for an hour, or more.
  Use as required.

OILS, VINEGARS AND SPIRITS

THYME VINEGAR

300 ml/10 fl oz/1^{1}/$_{4}$ cups white wine vinegar
4 sprigs fresh thyme on the stem

Warm the vinegar and two sprigs of thyme together in a saucepan for 5 minutes. Cool. Put the stems of thyme in a bottle and pour in the vinegar. Bottle and keep in a sunny place for 2–3 weeks. Strain, then rebottle using two sprigs of fresh thyme.

ROSEMARY AND BAY VINEGAR

300 ml/10 fl oz/1^{1}/$_{4}$ cups white wine vinegar
2 sprigs rosemary
8 bay leaves

Warm the vinegar, one sprig of rosemary and four bay leaves together in a saucepan for 5 minutes. Cool. Put the rosemary stem and the bay leaves in a bottle then pour in the vinegar. Bottle and keep in a sunny place for 2–3 weeks. Strain and rebottle using a sprig of fresh rosemary and four fresh bay leaves.

CHILLI AND PEPPER OLIVE OIL

1 large fresh red chilli, pricked all over
12 peppercorns
300 ml/10 fl oz/1^{1}/$_{4}$ cups olive oil

Place all the ingredients in a bottle and store for 3 weeks. Oils do not need to be strained.

SESAME, GARLIC AND GINGER OIL

2 cloves garlic
5 cm/2 in piece ginger, peeled and chopped
300 ml/10 fl oz/1^{1}/$_{4}$ cups sesame oil

Prepare as above.

CHILLI VODKA

4 whole chilli peppers
1 bottle (750 ml / 1¼ pints / 3 cups) vodka

Prick the chillies all over with the point of a knife, and place in the bottle of vodka.

Place in the freezer for at least 24 hours.

After 24 hours the vodka is ready for drinking. The longer you infuse the chillies, the stronger the heat. Remove chillies when the desired heat has been reached.

Serve in chilled shot glasses.

DAMSON OR SLOE GIN

1.2 litres / 2 pints / 5 cups gin
350 g / 12 oz / 1¾ cups granulated sugar
Few drops almond essence
450 g / 1 lb/3½ cups damsons or sloes, washed and dried

Put the gin, sugar and almond essence into a 2 litre/ 3½ pint/8 cup Kilner (preserving) jar. Prick the damsons or sloes and put into the gin mixture.

Seal the jar and leave to infuse for 3–4 months, shaking occasionally.

Strain and bottle the gin. Keep the fruit for use in flavourings. The flavour of the gin improves with keeping.

SPICE MIXTURES

QUATRE EPICES

Jamaica allspice
Cloves
Cinnamon or ginger
Pepper or nigella

Mix an equal amount of the ground spices together. Place the mixture in a clean glass jar or container and store in a cool, dark place.

INDIAN FIVE SPICE

Cumin seed
Fennel seed
Fenugreek seed
Nigella seed
Black mustard seed

Grind together equal amounts of the seeds. Store as above.

CHINESE FIVE SPICE

Star anise
Fennel seed
Cassia (Chinese cinnamon)
Cloves
Szechwan pepper

Grind together equal amounts of the spices. Store as above.

THE HISTORY OF THE SITE

'This could be a fantastic alternative to Covent Garden,
a place where creative activity could occur'

Sir Terence Conran

In the early days of its renaissance, reaching the Butlers Wharf Building could be a learning experience even if you'd been told the way: a PhD in geography helped. The site is bordered to the north by the River Thames, to the east by St Saviour's Dock and to the west by the ex-Courage Brewery abutting Tower Bridge; it extends southwards for several blocks into Southwark. These facts alone put it clearly on the *A to Z*. Even so, taxi drivers weren't always clear where it was: when the majority of the current crop did their 'knowledge' Butlers Wharf was derelict. Such has been the Gastrodrome's success, however, that the area is now firmly and famously back on the map.

For a foretaste of the labyrinthine streets that make up its hinterland – home patch of Charles Dickens's Bill Sykes – try the opening lines of chapter 50 of *Oliver Twist*:

To reach this place, the visitor has to penetrate through a maze of close, narrow, and muddy streets, thronged by the roughest and poorest of waterside people, and devoted to the traffic they may be supposed to occasion. The cheapest and least delicate provisions are heaped in the shops; the coarsest and commonest articles of wearing apparel dangle at the salesman's door . . . [the visitor] makes his way with difficulty along, assailed by offensive sights and smells from the narrow alleys which branch off on the right and left, and deafened by the clash of ponderous waggons that bear great piles of merchandise from the stacks of warehouses that rise from every corner . . .

What you find today is an upmarket version of Dickens's crowded scene, but it's recognizably the same corner of southeast London.

The Gastrodrome is merely the latest of many colourful developments that

Landing cases of ginger at Butlers Wharf at the turn of the century. The Wharf was also a major port for the importing of tea, rubber, and metals.

Butlers Wharf Ltd owned a fleet of horse-drawn vans to transport merchandise.

this site has witnessed since it was a marshy swamp in the Saxon era. In the thirteenth century, King John was allegedly thrown from his horse here, hence Horsleydown Lane, wedged in between Butlers Wharf and Tower Bridge. Until the Dissolution in 1536, Church-controlled Southwark was a den of thieves and murderers outside the jurisdiction of London and free from the direct control of the King. During the Counter-Reformation, French and Flemish Protestant refugees were drawn here. In the Elizabethan era, when the maritime trade routes opened up, the banks of the Thames sprouted wharfs as Southwark became a thriving shipbuilding centre.

Ownership of the site passed from Church to Crown and thence to landowners including Sir John Fastolf (who is said to have inspired Shakespeare's Falstaff) and the Thomas family who leased it out to sundry merchants, including one 'Mr Butler' in 1794. Nothing more can be gleaned from local records, except that Mr Butler was a merchant of some consequence.

Butlers Wharf was a thriving commercial port at the turn of the century. Here, tapioca imported from the West Indies is weighed in one of the offices.

In the nineteenth century wharfs gave way to today's tall Victorian warehouses as Butlers Wharf took in cargoes shipped from all outposts of the British Empire. At first there was only grain and tea, but later everything from rubber to nutmeg.

Modern containerized shipping killed off the area as a trading centre almost overnight as fully automated container terminals superseded wharfs. As the last East German freighter discharged its crated cargo in March 1972, the future looked bleak until, sixteen years later, the son of a rugby-playing commodities trader fell in love with Butlers Wharf and bought it.

As a boy, Terence Conran often visited Docklands with his father to watch ships from the Belgian Congo unload gum copal resin, a commodity in which Rupert Conran dealt. His father's base was in Stepney, where Terence recalls streets running with molten resin during the wartime bombing.

But as a designer he was always intrigued by transforming derelict or ex-industrial sites into places to live, work, shop and eat. In September 1979, Conran threw a staff party aboard a pleasure cruiser on the Thames. 'The boat came downriver to just beyond Tower Bridge,' he recalls, 'and turned in midstream. I was on deck, leaning on the guardrail, having a drink with a couple of senior designers. I looked up and there was Butlers Wharf, with all these buildings derelict and one end of the Butlers Wharf Building [then prosaically named Warehouse A-D] burnt out. This could be a fantastic alternative to Covent Garden, I thought, a place where architects and designers and creative activity could occur. I was worried that Covent Garden was becoming too tourist-ridden and expensive. There had already been talk of developing Docklands.'

The only on-site activity, besides rat-traffic and an artists' colony, was the spice-grinding company Butlers, Grinders & Operators which P&O owned. P&O were only too willing to sell off Butlers Wharf. A friend of Conran, the artist Stephen Buckley, happened to take a studio at the east end of the Butlers Wharf Building and another acquaintance, sculptor and jeweller Andrew Logan, lived in the Gold Room inside the Building and staged the Alternative Miss World there in 1975. David Hockney also lived there for a while. Otherwise it was a no-go area.

For months, Conran mulled over the site. But at this stage he had no plans for a gastronomic centre. Conran put in a mixed-use plan, won LDDC approval and in 1981 bought the freehold from P&O. Unsafe buildings were demolished and roads and drains laid down. Cinnamon Wharf and Butlers Wharf Pier were built, and Conran contacted companies that might relocate. He also moved the Design Museum from the Victoria & Albert Museum in South Kensington to its present site, described by Conran as 'an appalling 1950s structure . . . it would have been cheaper to have demolished it,' he says. 'But we saved VAT by stripping it down to its skeleton and reconstructing it.'

Although the Design Museum is not part of the Gastrodrome, moving it to Butlers Wharf fitted Conran's idea of a 'destination' that embraced culture.

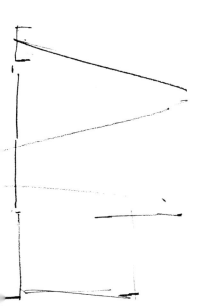

A view from Butlers Wharf of Tower Bridge raised to allow passage to the *Belle* steamer.

'Perhaps that thought was in advance of its time,' he says. 'Interesting to note that in 2000 the Tate Gallery will expand to Bankside a few yards upstream.' The Design Museum opened in July 1989.

When interest rates rose in the late 1980s, London property values deteriorated. But Conran, emboldened by the sell-out of Cinnamon Wharf next to St Saviour's Dock, was committed to reconstructing the vast Butlers Wharf Building itself, a Grade II listed edifice on a conservation site.

The idea of a gastronomic centre was still a long way off, but there were vague plans to open a restaurant. Conran invited the Roux Brothers, Anton Mosimann and Marchesi Lodovico Antinori to open restaurants and wine bars in the Butlers Wharf Building. One by one they turned him down. Jean Paul Bucher, the Parisian brasserie owner, thought of opening in Spice Quay (now the car park), then withdrew. Justin de Blank looked around, shook his head and left. Even Giles Shepard, then MD of the Savoy Group, considered opening a hotel but swiftly changed his mind. By 1990 Conran's vision of Butlers Wharf

Revisited was in tatters, well before the recession started scaring off investors in earnest and forcing banks to unplug credit lines.

Unabashed, Conran opened the Blue Print Café on the mezzanine floor of the Design Museum. It had a difficult start. There was no disguising that it was in the middle of a building site, and within one year both chef and manager had left. One bright spot was that people who worked in the City and Docklands trekked across the river and along the riverfront in droves, defying experts who said they'd never 'go south' to eat.

The genesis of the Gastrodrome dates back to the period in 1989–90, when Conran was redesigning the interior of the Butlers Wharf Building. Poring over plans, he tossed around ideas for a smart two-level Bibendum-style restaurant called Le Pont de la Tour with its own bakery, food store and wine merchant. A far cry from the hastily improvised Blue Print Café, Le Pont de la Tour was intended to be a large 'destination' restaurant that would draw people to the area. The downstream end of the Butlers Wharf Building – now occupied by Cantina del Ponte – was pinpointed as the most promising site, and huge ventilation ducts were installed.

To organize the construction, setting up and running of Le Pont de la Tour, Conran appointed Joel Kissin, a 36-year-old Bibendum manager from New Zealand whose youthful mien belies nerves of titanium. 'For nearly a year I sat in a makeshift office in a studio flat in the Butlers Wharf Building surrounded by piles of paper and no secretary,' says Kissin. 'I negotiated a lease with the help of a solicitor.'

Then Conran and Kissin had a change of plan. It was decided to switch Le Pont de la Tour from being a two-level restaurant at one end of the Butlers Wharf Building to a larger ground-floor restaurant in the middle of the building, where it could be opened directly on to the public walkway linking Shad Thames to the riverfront. Adding the bar and grill to Le Pont de la Tour seemed a huge gamble, given that so many of Conran's other plans for Butlers Wharf were in jeopardy because of the deepening recession. Indeed, barely had

Sketch by Terence Conran for the ladies' lavatories at Le Pont de la Tour.

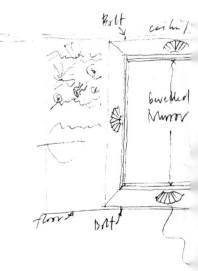

the finishing touches been made to the planning and layout of the new-look Le Pont de la Tour in December 1990 than the receivers* were called in.

Most businessmen might have washed their hands of Butlers Wharf. But Conran clung on. His offices were on site and he had little desire to leave. If only in self-justification, he claims he never intended Butlers Wharf to make piles of money. 'It was a sideline,' he insists. The company had done nothing worse than be wrong-footed by recession, and to have its opportunities for optimism dampened by prevailing City gloom. Even the banks consoled him by saying Butlers Wharf was one of the more *successful* projects of its ilk.

Risking a substantial amount of his own money, Conran did what seemed the least sensible thing: to carry on with opening Le Pont de la Tour. Plans for the restaurant were ready except for the aesthetics – the finishes, the colour schemes, the artwork and the pictures – which had yet to be decided on and commissioned. But firstly the lease had to be renegotiated with the receivers. 'I walked into a hastily called meeting to find seven people from Butlers Wharf receivers sitting opposite me,' says Joel Kissin. 'I was by myself. There hadn't even been time to call a lawyer. They said, "We're throwing out the deal you've done. We'll have to renegotiate the lease." I said, "Thank you very much," got up and left. I had to walk out of two more meetings before they realized I was serious about opening a restaurant. In their eyes it was a daft idea, but I knew that if nothing happened, I'd be out of a job, with no money, and I would probably have gone into a different career. It was tough.'

'I felt that if we were going to do it,' Conran muses in retrospect, 'we should do it with a huge amount of confidence and in a way that really made a mark. If I'd gone timorously into an itsy-bitsy restaurant, it probably wouldn't have succeeded. But if you do something with real confidence, extremely well and make a big noise about it, people notice.'

In a whirlwind six months, Kissin appointed David Burke (ex-sous chef at Bibendum) as head chef and hired staff, whilst Conran briefed his team of designers on fitting out the interior of Le Pont de la Tour to his instructions.

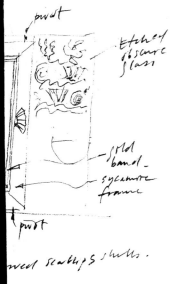

* The Butlers Wharf Building is now owned by the Danish Trades Union Pension Fund K.P. Bolig-Byg I A/S.

Under the umbrella term 'the Gastrodrome', Le Pont de la Tour, the Food Store, the Wine Merchant, the Bar and Grill and the Bakery, opened on 23 September 1991 followed days later by a firework display and cabaret put on by Conran's children to celebrate their father's sixtieth birthday. 'It was crazy,' recalls Kissin. 'For the first three days we offered half-price previews. We were swamped. Computers, fridges and coolers broke down, so people were left without food. Terence was very, very nervous. We had terrible fights. He went spare one evening shortly after we opened when he was entertaining important friends and the computer system went down.'

'One year later when we were about to open Cantina del Ponte,' says Kissin, 'I sat Terence down and said, "What I need from you is to be unfailingly cheerful. It will help if you please keep smiling." Ever since then, he has realized that when he makes a fuss, everything freezes.'

Had Le Pont de la Tour failed, Conran's plans for Butlers Wharf might have been terminated and he might have retreated to the countryside 'to make furniture'. But the press gave excellent reviews, and the City descended en masse both at lunch and dinner. Just a short walk across from the battery-henhouse dealing rooms and the rugby-scrum wine bars of the Square Mile, this luxurious restaurant seemed like a haven where one could eat, drink and execute high-powered deals in a climate of the utmost respectability. 'That it was outside the City was exactly why I knew it would work,' says Conran. 'The City has one code inside the Square Mile, another outside.' Perhaps the year he spent shuttling between financial analysts, institutional shareholders and banks while at Storehouse was not entirely in vain.

There were no immediate plans for further restaurants. 'Our ambitions didn't go any further than Le Pont de la Tour, its Bakery, Food Store and Wine Merchant,' says Conran. 'We felt we were being pretty daring.' But the success of Le Pont de la Tour was a boost. Quietly, Conran began formulating ideas for a family of restaurants and shops that would help turn Butlers Wharf into the destination that he had dreamt about.

ELEVATION Scale 1:50

Exterior elevation and kitchen floorplan for the Butlers Wharf Chop-house.

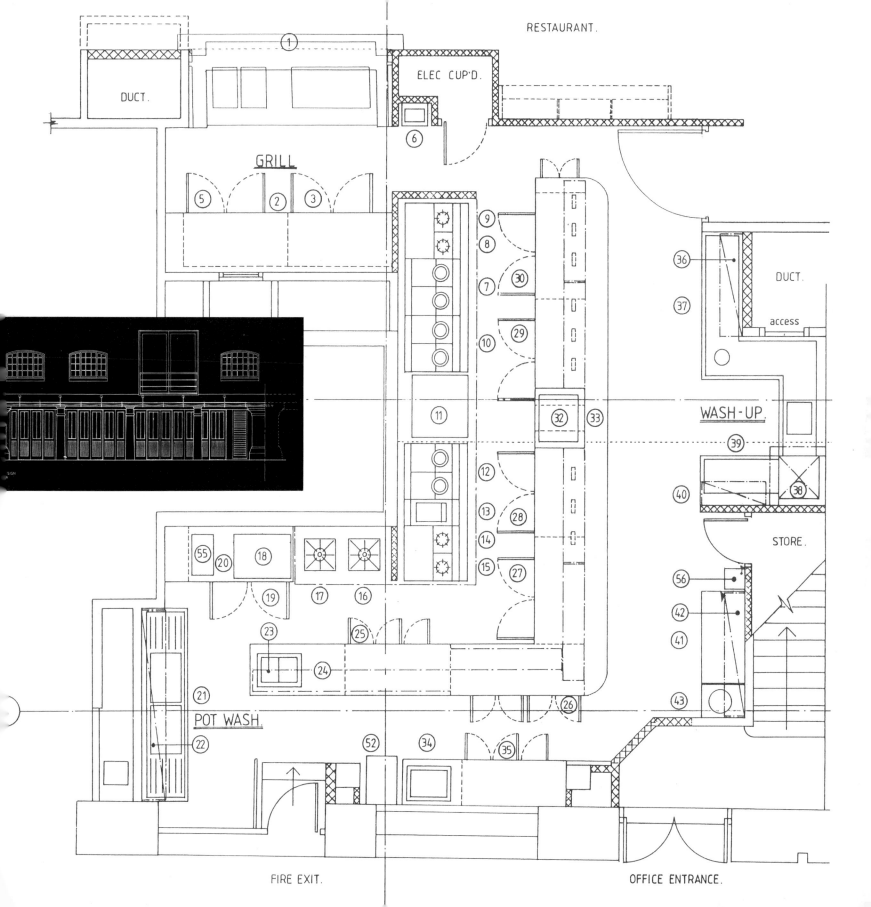

RESTAURANT.

DUCT.

ELEC CUP'D.

① 6

GRILL

⑤ ② ③

DUCT.

access

⑨
⑧
⑦ ㉚
⑩ ㉙

㊱
㊲

⑪ ㉜ ㉝

WASH-UP.

㊴

⑫

㊳
㊵

⑬ ㉘

⑮ ㉗
⑭

STORE.

㊶ ㉝

⑤⑤ ⑳ ⑱ ⑤⑥
㉔
⑲ ⑰ ⑯ ㊷
㊶
㉓ ㉕
㉑ ㉔ ㊸
㉖

POT WASH.

㉒ ㊸ ㉔ ㉟

FIRE EXIT.

OFFICE ENTRANCE.

INDEX OF RECIPES

ACKNOWLEDGEMENTS

The author and publishers would like to thank the following for allowing them
to reproduce copyright material:

David Brittain for the photographs on pages 3 (left); 70, 71, 72, 73, 74–5, 81,
126, 128 (top and bottom)

Simon Brown for the photographs on pages 8, 14–15, 15 (right), 17, 25 and 29;

Butlers Wharf Limited for the photographs on pages 144, 146–7, 148, 149,
151 and 155

Terence Conran for the illustrations on pages 46–7, 150–1, and 152–3;

Helen Drew for the photographs on pages 3 (right), 10 (right), 11, 23, 47, 61,
94, 96–7, 97 (right), 99 (top), 100, 101, 102–3, 109, 110, 124 (top and
bottom), 129 (top and bottom) and 130;

Ken Kirkwood for the photographs on pages 2 (right), 38, 40, 41, 42, 43,
44 (left), 44–5, 46, 48–9, 51, 122, 132 and 143–5;

Roger Stowell for the photographs on pages 2 (left), 5, 9 (left and right),
10 (left), 12, 16, 18–19, 21, 22, 27, 31, 34, 36, 53, 55, 56, 57, 58, 63, 67, 68,
77, 79, 82, 85, 86, 87, 90, 93, 98, 99 (bottom), 107, 113, 115, 117, 119,
120–1 and 131.